Good, Better, Best

The Rags-to-Riches Story of the Upscale Resale Queen

Good Better

Best

The Rags-to-Riches Story of the Upscale Resale Queen

Sue McCarthy

Star of the Style Network's *Resale Royalty*

with Diana McCarthy Ford and Laura McCarthy Maurice

Dedication

For the strong women in my life, Dorothy and Susanna, who taught me early on, "As a man thinketh, so a man is." They were the most positive women I've ever known, and they taught me that anything is possible if you just put your miraculous mind to it. This is for you.

Acknowledgments

I am very grateful to my daughters, Diana and Laura, for their help with this book and for sharing this great adventure with me.

I'd like to thank my husband, Larry, for his love and unwavering support.

Finally, I'd like to thank my editor and friend, Stephanie Abbajay. Without her editorial guidance and diligence in keeping us on track, this book never would have come to fruition.

The Hummingbird

As I sat with the beads of the Rosary between my fingers,
the decades resting in my heart,
I watched a hummingbird speedily buzzing
from flower to flower to flower.

It went back and forth for a few minutes as I watched,
its wings almost invisible with strength.

Then suddenly, for just a few moments, it stopped —
stopped flying, stopped flitting, stopped seeking;
Just stopped.

Turning its face to mine, it sat
unnervingly still, breathtakingly quiet
before it disappeared from my sight.

Left only was its energy,
on every beautiful flower,
on every wisp of air its wings took in —
its dazzling ruby energy written in my memory forever.

And what a powerful and profound energy it will be.

~ Anna Mullens

Note to readers

Our business is based on integrity. We guarantee the authenticity of every item we sell, and we guarantee the confidentiality of our suppliers. In chapter eight, we use the real names of the clients who appeared on our TV Show, *Resale Royalty*. Elsewhere, the names and identifying characteristics of suppliers and clients have been changed.

Chapter One
The Luckiest Woman in the World

It's a beautiful spring day. Warm sunlight is streaming through giant windows. I can hear the ocean waves lap against the shore. I hear a maid quietly padding about in the other room. I hear the hushed but excited chatter of my two daughters as they peruse the designer garments we've been invited to look at in this massive, bespoke walk-in closet. It belongs to one of the East Coast's wealthiest and most recognizable women, a New York socialite who has invited us to her beachfront East Hamptons mansion to look through and possibly buy her items for our boutique in Saint Louis, the Vault Luxury Resale.

As I look at the racks of gorgeous clothes, I am suddenly transported back in time to another spring day, a spring day of my childhood. The memory comes to me in a flash, clear as a bell: I am four years old, in a dusty church basement in New Orleans, digging through piles of cast-off clothing with my mother, searching for Easter outfits for me and my siblings. We are homeless and hungry, and my mother and I are grateful for the opportunity to look through bins of free clothes, items discarded by others but new and exciting to us.

My daughters' voices snap me back to the present day. I look around and take stock. Here I am jet-setting across the country to meet some of the world's wealthiest women and go through their incredible closets. Here I am sorting through couture gowns, Hermès scarves, and Chanel jewelry in a sun-filled mansion in the Hamptons.

I close my eyes and see myself again in that dark church basement, giddy after finding a dress. It was a little worse for wear, but to me it was a ball gown. Back then, food and shelter were the priorities — new clothes were never an option. Today, my shoes cost more than my father made in a month. I lean against the wall and take a few deep breaths. I've come a long way, baby.

Imagine a store that has all the world's finest luxury brands under one roof and at prices that almost every woman can afford: Chanel, Dior, Hermès. Yves Saint Laurent, Marc Jacobs. Prada, Fendi, Gucci. Louis Vuitton, Michael Kors. Stella McCartney, Eileen Fisher. Kate Spade. David Yurman, Ralph Lauren, Calvin Klein. Jimmy Choo, Christian Louboutin, Manolo Blahnik.

Those are the labels that my daughters and I proudly sell at our shop — the Vault Luxury Resale. We are one of the country's leading resellers of high-end designer items. We buy and sell clothing, shoes, handbags, and accessories from the world's top brands. From couture to ready-to-wear, we buy and sell the labels that every woman in the world wants.

And it's not all Chanel. We also buy and sell popular brands like Coach, J. Crew, Banana Republic, Theory, Vince, Tory Burch, Free People, Eileen Fisher, Kate Spade, Rebecca Taylor, and Lululemon. If it's high fashion, high quality, high style, and au courant, we buy it. We are the reigning queens of upscale resale.

As many know from our 2013 Style Network reality TV series, *Resale Royalty*, we pay on the spot for clothes, shoes, accessories, and handbags. We authenticate every item, and we resell those items to an adoring, dedicated, and massive customer base, which waits patiently (and sometimes not so patiently) to see what new items we have. If you can't find what you want in our store, just wait; eventually, that piece you've been searching for or didn't even know you wanted will turn up, in perfect condition and at an unbelievable price. The Vault is a shopper's dream, a fashionista's delight. We are a girl's best friend. And, because of this, we are phenomenally successful.

Our recipe for success is simple: We find out what people want, and we give it to them with honesty and integrity at a fair price. We get the good jeans because we've got the best genes in the business. We know what we're doing. What sets us apart is that we are the best in three very important categories: quality, quantity, and price. We treat our suppliers and our customers like royalty. We think fashion should be affordable. We think every woman deserves to look great and wear nice things, regardless of size or income. And we deliver on that promise.

How do we do it? We carefully curate our inventory, buying only the best items. We say, "No, thank you" to as many items as we say, "Yes, please!" Everything we sell is in perfect condition and ready to wear. About 30 percent of our items still have the price tags on them, so they have literally never been worn. We have a roster of over 15,000 suppliers, from the US and all over the world, from whom we take in and process over 500 items a day. We move a massive amount of merchandise, so shoppers always find something "new" and fabulous at the Vault.

Our store is beautiful and elegant, and we treat our customers like family. Care for a glass of champagne? A cup of coffee? An ice-cold bottle of water? How about relaxing for a few minutes on one of our overstuffed sofas? Going on a trip or have a special event? We'll have one of our personal shoppers pull a rack of items for you.

We have one simple goal: Find out what people want and give it to them. This has made the Vault one of the most successful resale shops in the country.

We also provide a very special service for very special clients: the closet buy. You see, we buy items from women from all walks of life: Housewives, college students, professionals, stay-at-home moms, soccer moms, working women, fashionistas, you name it. But we also have a roster of suppliers who move in very different circles: international jet setters, movie stars, celebrities and their stylists, socialites, famous designers, the super wealthy, the one percenters. We buy from the girls next door and from the world's wealthiest women alike. And sometimes we buy from the mistresses, girlfriends, and escorts of the world's wealthiest men. We don't judge. We just buy the best items that are for sale.

Many of our suppliers prefer to sell in the privacy of their homes, for various reasons. They may be too famous to walk into our store in Saint Louis, schlepping shopping bags full of Prada shoes and Gucci belts. Or they may be too busy. Or—and we love these the best—they may have so many items that they couldn't possibly come in. Those are the closet buys. If you can't come to us, because you're too famous or too busy or you have too much merchandise, we'll gladly come to you—after we verify that you've got the goods, of course. We do that with phone calls, photos, and proof that what you have to sell is worth our time and travel.

We look at hundreds of closets a year here in Saint Louis, across the country, and abroad as well. The transactions are usually simple, and we're generally in and out in under an hour. But occasionally we encounter a closet so extraordinary, so spectacular, that it becomes the stuff of legend. Those closets are full of fantastic finds, and there are unbelievable stories that go with them. And those are the closet buys we'll share with you. We've gone to Paris for Birkin bags, Vegas for Versace, Chicago for Jimmy Choo, Milan for Prada. We've gone all over the world buying the most amazing luxury items, and we've seen the world's best closets. And I'm here to tell you, they are amazing. The stories we can tell you! Actually, the stories we *are* going to tell you!

I'm the luckiest woman in the world. I get to do what I love—buy beautiful things *and* share them with the world—with the people I love most—my two daughters, who are my partners at the Vault. Together, the three of us travel the globe in search of the most beautiful items so we can resell them to our wonderful, loyal customers. I believe that beautiful things are meant to be shared. And if it's not becoming on you, it should be coming to me.

The story of the Vault is the story of my life, and it's literally a story of rags to riches. From being homeless and penniless as a child to owning one of the top luxury resale businesses in the country, *Good, Better, Best* tells the story of my life, takes you inside the world's most fabulous closets, and goes behind the scenes of luxury resale. There are tips and tricks of the trade, stories of amazing closet buys, ups and downs, and successes and failures.

My success today is the result of thousands of buys, thousands of sales, and lots of mistakes. I've learned from my mistakes and moved forward bigger and better than ever. I've learned that failure just means that you found something that doesn't work. That's how you get ahead, how you learn, and how you succeed. At least that's how I did it.

Many women dream of owning items from the world's best brands. Many women fantasize about owning a spectacular walk-in closet full of the most gorgeous clothes money can buy. Those are the closets we get into.

Come with us as we go into the world's most fabulous closets and come out with amazing items. Come with us behind the scenes of upscale resale. Learn the tricks of the trade, meet our buyers and suppliers, and enjoy *Good, Better, Best*.

Chapter Two
From Rags to Riches

Chanel, Gucci, Hermès, Louis Vuitton. Those names are as recognizable to me now as the names of my own children. Those and other luxury labels fly off the shelves and racks of my shop, the Vault Luxury Resale.

But those names were not at all familiar to me as a child growing up in the 1950s. The labels I knew then were of a different sort: poor, hungry, and homeless. I wore rummage-sale clothes and shoes stuffed with newspaper and cardboard to cover the holes in the soles. The first house I remember living in had no indoor plumbing. My beginnings were as humble as you can imagine, and I do not for one minute take for granted the life I now live.

As I write this, I'm comfortably ensconced on my custom overstuffed sofa in my well-appointed house in Webster Groves, Missouri, with my Ferragamo-clad feet propped up on my French coffee table (neither of which I paid retail for, mind you). I've traveled the world for business and pleasure, to search for the finest items to sell in my stores and to take in the sights. I have spa'd at Miraval, cocktailed with Valentino, dined with Deepak Chopra, and had high tea at Harrod's in London.

I work every day doing something I love—buying and selling luxury goods—with the people I love most, my two daughters, Diana and Laura. It's the thrill of the hunt and the "get," and we work side-by-side bringing affordable luxury to women everywhere. I have everything my heart desires.

But as a child, I had nothing. And that's not an exaggeration. When I was four years old, my family lived in a park. I don't mean we spent weekends camping in a park or had picnics in a park. No, we actually lived in a park. It was 1951, and we were homeless.

I was born in 1947 in Saint Louis, Missouri. My parents, Oscar and Dorothy Ashlock, were both children of the Great Depression who grew up with itinerate lifestyles. You lived where there was a place to sleep, you worked wherever you found it, and you took care of your family as best you could. They met in the 1940s during the war. My mother worked at a small arms ammunition plant, and my father was in the Army. Dorothy rode a motorcycle, smoked cigarettes, and wore pants, all of which was pretty risqué for the time. She was a real Rosie the Riveter, and Oscar fell in love with her independent, adventurous spirit.

After the war, housing was scarce and jobs were hard to find. It wasn't that unusual for people to live with their parents, and, after they married, Oscar and Dorothy lived with his family. My grandparents had a very full house, with seven of their adult children, including my father and mother, living with them. In five years, my parents had three kids and another one on the way.

That seemed like the perfect time to set out on their own, so my dad bought a piece of property in the country, and we camped there with a tent and a lean-to for a year. When he finally dug the foundation and built the basement, we moved in even though it was without indoor plumbing or electricity. We had an outhouse.

The property was next to a creek, which is where we washed dishes, bathed, and got our drinking water. We lived there for two years. I remember sweltering summers and freezing winters. We were like pioneers, my three siblings, my parents, and me, exposed to the elements and making the best of everything. I don't remember those as desperate days, though. Thanks to my mother and her indomitable spirit, everything was a great adventure. She was so good to us and made us feel like life was great fun. I also didn't know any different. I bloomed where I was planted. That's the way I was raised, and that's how I lived.

My father took care of us the best he could. In his world, however, children were seen and not heard, and we weren't allowed to complain or be sick. And he didn't believe in doctors. At the first sign of a sniffle or sore throat, he would yell, "Mother, get the vinegar!" And my mother would put together the Vinegar Treatment—apple cider vinegar, baking soda, and a little sugar. We would have to drink that any time we were suspected of being the slightest bit sick or injured. Any ailment, from a fever to a sprained ankle, got the treatment. Even though it wasn't that bad, we didn't exactly look forward to it.

It was never just us. My father had nine siblings, and he helped take care of them as well. There was always someone else living with us—an aunt and uncle, cousins, you name it. I spent my childhood sleeping on rollaway beds in the kitchen or on cots on the floor wherever there was extra space, always sharing what little bed I had. I didn't sleep alone in my own bed until I was a teenager. There was always another family living with us, more mouths to feed, more people to take care of. It was a huge drain on my father's resources, but he did the best he could.

My father was a very proud man. He always felt there was something better he could or should be doing, something better somewhere for his family. He always strove for better, better, better. His motto, the motto that was drummed into my head constantly as a child, was, "Good, better, best. Never let it rest until the good is the better and the better is the best." That motto would come to define my working ethos later in life. Never stop trying to improve. Never rest on your laurels. Never take the easy way out. Always strive for better. "Good, better, best" were the words I lived by. And still do.

In my father's endless search for better, we moved around. *A lot*. In truth, we were very poor and always were. It never got better with my dad. But we were proud and didn't believe in welfare. If you didn't have food to eat, you just didn't eat. If you didn't have a place to live, you lived in your car or in a park. We never took anything from anybody, and my father did whatever he could to make money.

That usually took the form of going wherever he could to find work. In Saint Louis, the best place to work back then was Anheuser-Busch. He worked there for a while and did well, but the work was seasonal, and he was never able to get hired full time.

One day, my dad heard that they were hiring welders for new oilrigs in New Orleans. So, in 1951, when I was four years old, he packed us up, and we headed south. My dad announced we were moving, and that was that.

We all piled into the old Ford and drove straight to New Orleans. We arrived with no money, nowhere to live, and no job; turns out, the jobs were not as plentiful as he had heard. We drove around the wealthier neighborhoods, where my dad went door-to-door asking for work—yard work, car repair, handyman services, any work he could get. We kids and my mother sat in the car, and, as he spoke to the people at the door, my father would motion to us to let people know he had a family to support. He was always able to get some kind of work.

He settled us in a park until he was able to make enough to rent an apartment. It was one of those big, beautiful parks that New Orleans is famous for, with huge old trees dripping with moss. I remember thinking it was absolutely magical, so different from Saint Louis.

That first day we had a ball. We played all day in the park with the neighborhood kids, having a blast. But when darkness fell, all the kids went home to their houses, their suppers, and their beds. I got scared and worried, and I said to my mother, "Mom, all the kids are going home. Where are we going to sleep tonight?"

Even in the lean-to, even in the house with no plumbing or walls, we had always had a place to sleep. My mother told me, "They all have to go home, but we are lucky. We get to stay here all night long. And we'll be the first ones on the swings in the morning."

And just like that she set the theme and the tone for the rest of my life. She shifted my perspective from focusing on the negative to seeing the best in every situation. We didn't have to go home to sleep—we got to sleep in the park! We weren't homeless—we were on an adventure! She made us feel as if we were the lucky ones. That's what my mother did for us. She made the very best of everything, of every situation, no matter the reality. To this day, I know who I am because of my mother. She taught me to change my view, to shift my thinking, to always look for the positive, and to keep my energy and spirits up. Bloom where you're planted.

In many ways, my mother was in her glory. As a child of the Depression, she grew up with nothing, and she delighted in how little she needed to get by. She both adored and rose to the challenge of raising four kids with no money or help. She never complained. She was a simple woman who never wanted for material things. She was resilient and courageous and full of confidence, and she passed her courage and feelings of self-worth along to us.

These were survival skills imparted to us by a woman trying her best to keep her children safe and sound. As much as she wanted us to believe we were on an adventure, the truth was that my father, though an absolutely charming man, was a poor provider. He had a generous heart of gold, and he talked a good game, but he was irresponsible and bad with money. My mother did the best she could to make us see everything as an adventure rather than what it really was—a terrible situation, a family destitute and on the verge of collapse. The truth was that we were homeless and penniless, with nowhere to turn.

We lived in the park for a few weeks. Every night, after all the kids and their families had gone home and it was getting dark, my mother would lay out blankets for us. If we had food, she would divvy it up. Sometimes it was just a loaf of bread. Sometimes we had a little salami or bologna. Sometimes all we had was bruised fruit or vegetables or a few cans of beans or peas. We would lie down under the stars and eat what little we had. My mother would tell us stories until we fell asleep. We would rise very early to the sound of traffic and the noises of the city and wash up in the public bathrooms and fountains.

But being poor in my world was just a state of mind. We never thought of ourselves as poor because my parents had convinced us we were on a grand adventure. Plus, there were lots of people just like us. We weren't the only people sleeping in the park and bathing in the fountain. This was the early 1950s. It was still postwar America, and not everyone was back on their feet. And air-conditioning wasn't a modern convenience yet; lots of people slept in the park because it was cooler, so we were by no means alone, and I never thought of myself as poor.

All day we'd play in the park while my dad walked up and down the streets, knocking on doors to find work. He'd fix cars, buff out dents, rake leaves, mow yards, whatever it took to feed his family. Finally, he saved enough money to rent a furnished apartment in Algiers, an African-American community in New Orleans on the west bank of the Mississippi River. We were one of the only white families in the area, but we were welcomed with open arms.

We lived next door to a funeral parlor, and it seemed like there was a funeral every day. And when there's a funeral in New Orleans, there's a band and a parade. It's a celebration. We'd come out of our basement apartment and sit on the sidewalk and watch the parade. It was fabulous. I learned to look at life differently from that experience. Death doesn't seem so scary when there's a parade and a party involved.

We were so different from the people we lived around. We were the outsiders, but we were treated with love and kindness. Living in New Orleans, I learned that life was an adventure. I learned not to judge people because of their skin color. I learned to have an open heart and to be open to new people and experiences.

That's also where I first learned sales. My father was a natural-born salesman. Whether he was selling vegetables door-to-door or his services as a handyman, he was always impeccable in his appearance and manners. He was very handsome and always presented himself as a nice young man whom everyone wanted as a friend or to do business with. We all inherited a natural ability for sales from him, and he taught us the ropes. (As adults, every one of his children owned his or her own business. I think Dad would have been proud of us.)

My first job was selling vegetables out of the back of his truck. Five days a week, we went to the farmer's market at 4 a.m. to collect our fruits and vegetables. We would drive up and down the streets yelling, "Fresh fruits and vegetables! Get your vegetables right off the vine!" People would yell from their window what they wanted. I would put the items in a brown paper bag and bring it to the door. I always collected an extra nickel or dime because here I was, this cute little girl working with her dad. I loved the attention, and I quickly learned the terrific effect of a genuine smile and being polite.

And that's where I first learned of *lagniappe*, which means a bonus or little something extra. My dad said, "Susie, we are in New Orleans where lanyap [that's what it sounded like when he said it] is a way of life. You will find that a nice smile, a polite attitude, and giving the customer a little extra something is the key to doing great business. That's lagniappe in a nut-shell." That's what we gave every person we met, and that's exactly what I still do to this day—give my customers a little something extra. Whether it's extra attention or a gracious welcoming attitude, bottles of water or glasses of Champagne, lagniappe, that little bonus, is a cornerstone of my business.

My dad knew what he was doing. He always made sure I looked as cute as possible, because he always made more money that way. The night before work, he would say, "Susie, we are going to the market in the morning, so get your beauty sleep!"

My dad was a real charmer. Despite our poverty, he was meticulous in his grooming and clothing. He had an instinctive sense of style, and I think I got my passion for fashion and style from him. We scoured church rummage sales and thrift stores wherever we went. Dad was always the first in line with us, and we were taught what to look for.

My mother would mend, clean, and press everything we got, and we were always the best-dressed kids in school, despite the fact that we wore cast-offs. (When we lived in the lean-to by the creek, my mother would heat an iron over hot coals to press our clothes.) I learned that you didn't have to spend a lot to look good and dress well. We had style, and my dad knew that if you looked good, you felt good. He also knew that people would respond more favorably to a well-dressed man, woman, or child.

I loved working with my dad. I got to meet so many people and see so many new parts of town, and I got to help him earn money. That was heady stuff for a child. I loved it. Working was in my blood, and from that moment on—the age of four—I have worked ever since. I always wanted to make money, and I was good at getting people to like me and buy things. I was also great at getting people to follow me, so I always had a gang around me. I would come up with some scheme to make money—selling old calendars or greeting cards or flowers we'd picked—and we'd go door-to-door. I could sell anything to anyone. I loved the challenge, and I adored making money for myself and my family. And I wanted to make my father proud of me.

A word about my father. On the surface, he was a wonderful man, charming and adventurous. We adored him, and we craved his attention and affection. But he was an abusive alcoholic, with terrifying mood swings. When he drank, which wasn't that often because we had so little money, he was terribly abusive to my mother and us kids. We learned at a very early age to stay out of his way when he drank. My mother protected us the best she could, and my older sister would lock us in a closet to keep us safe. But we heard what he did to our mother, and we knew first-hand what it felt like when he caught one of us. My older brother and I got the worst of it. We would be playing in the yard, and he'd say, "Come in here now." And if we hesitated for one moment, he would pull off his belt and beat us.

The next day, he was always very sorry, promising that it would never happen again. But, of course, it did. Like many children of abusive parents, we blamed ourselves for his behavior. We were too loud, too selfish. We ate too much food or made too many demands. I wanted to work hard so that he would be proud of me. I thought the abuse would stop if he saw what a good job I was doing.

It wasn't until years later that I realized that he had a disease and that it wasn't our fault. I know my father loved us, but the abuse he heaped on us was unconscionable. His drinking tore at our family in ways I never fully appreciated until I was an adult with a family of my own.

I started school that fall. I was only four years old, but my mother told the school district I was five so she could get me out of the house. Even with no money I dressed beautifully, and I became fast friends with a little girl whose father was a banker. One day, she invited me to dinner. My mother worked feverishly all afternoon to mend and iron an adorable dress she had found for me in a thrift shop. I washed up, put on my "new" dress, and my father drove me over to my friend's house on the other side of town. It was a nice, normal house, but coming from our basement apartment, I thought it was a palace. It was the nicest house I'd ever been in. My friend had her own bedroom—her own bedroom!—with her very own bed. I had never seen such luxury.

We had dinner in the dining room. We'd never had a house or an apartment with a dining room, and I'd never been in one before. I was desperate for them to like me, so I was on my best behavior, a real little lady. But my friend and her brother started fighting at the dinner table, throwing things at each other and screaming. At one point, the brother flung his fork at his sister, and it stuck right in the middle of her forehead. She screamed bloody murder, and I remember I started to cry because I was so afraid that I'd be asked to leave and never invited back.

We never stayed anywhere very long. We left Algiers after about two years, and we kept moving. Over the next seven years, we moved from New Orleans to Oklahoma to Granite City, Illinois, then back to Saint Louis. By the time I got to high school, I had been in six grade schools. I was always the new girl, and I learned at an early age that if I wanted to have any friends, I had to have a bubbling personality, to give that little something extra, that *lagniappe*. My older sister Diane was considered the beauty of the family, so I learned to play up my personality. I had learned from my father how to attract positive attention to help with sales, so I used the same techniques. I dressed well and learned to be a dynamic, one-person party. I learned to be fun, pleasant, and popular with a great, positive attitude. It served me well. It still serves me well!

In 1960, when I was thirteen, my father died suddenly of a heart attack. His seven sisters came to the funeral and each one, overcome with grief, collapsed or fainted in front of the coffin. It was quite a scene.

I loved my father, but I honestly felt an enormous sense of relief when he died. Over the years his drinking had escalated to the point where none of us could take it any longer. It was so bad that my older siblings left home as soon as they possibly could: My brother Randy joined the Navy and left home at seventeen, and my sister Diane got married and moved out when she was sixteen. I was thirteen and my younger brother John was nine, so we still lived at home. My father had spiraled into alcoholism and despair, and he died an old man at the age of forty-three.

We were stunned to learn that my father had a $2,000 life insurance policy. My mother didn't spend it on herself though. She gave $500 to each of us, and that was a lot of money back then. She saved mine and John's until we were old enough to do something with it.

After I finished eighth grade that year, my mother, John, and I jumped in her car for a cross-country road trip to visit Randy at his naval base in California. We had virtually no money, so we stopped along the way at what looked like decent restaurants, where my mother found work washing dishes or waiting tables to earn money for the next leg of the trip. We certainly didn't have money for a motel, so we slept in the car.

While my mother worked, John and I stayed in the car or walked around whatever town we were in, passing the time as best we could. I learned to drive that summer, too, and I remember long stretches of highway, windows down, radio on, smoking cigarettes, and piloting the family vehicle while my mother and brother slept in the back seat. I remember the look on people's faces as they passed me on the highway, a grinning thirteen-year-old at the wheel, having the time of her life.

When we got back to Saint Louis at the end of the summer, I started high school and two new jobs. I worked at a dime store at Lafayette and Jefferson, and I sold shoes at Soulard Market. I would parade up and down the aisles at Soulard in ridiculous high heels, showing off the wares. When I turned fifteen I got a job at White Castle on Kingshighway and Natural Bridge Road. I was a carhop, and we wore tight little fitted pants and a cute little hat. The uniforms were adorable because they wanted us to look good (lagniappe!).

I worked at that White Castle all through high school. When I turned sixteen, the boys started paying attention to me. A group of them used to come in and flirt with me, and we would all go out together as a group. One night, a big group of us were out. We parked somewhere and were hopping from car to car, visiting and listening to music. I was in the backseat of a car talking with a girlfriend, when the car door opened, the dome light came on, and standing there was the most gorgeous man I'd ever seen.

He looked just like George Peppard in *Breakfast at Tiffany's*. His name was Larry McCarthy, and when that door opened I looked at him and thought, "That's the man I'm going to marry." I knew instantly he was the one. I was smitten. Larry was a complete gentleman. He was different from the other boys. He was kind and quiet and stable, everything I wanted in a man. But the most attractive thing about Larry was his integrity. Even though it was a new concept for me, I recognized it immediately. Plus, he was a hunk, built like a prize fighter.

Larry and I dated all through high school. After I graduated, I used the $500 from my father's life insurance policy to enroll in beauty school in Saint Louis. And as soon as I graduated from beauty school in 1966, Larry and I got married.

I had to take my state boards down in the capital, Jefferson City, so that's where we honeymooned. We took a Greyhound bus from Saint Louis to Jeff City. We stayed in a hotel, my very first experience in one. It was a Best Western, but it felt like the Ritz to me. I felt like I was in the lap of luxury and that my new life, as a married woman and a real adult, was just beginning. I was nineteen and on my way.

I loved being married. Larry had a good job at General Motors in Saint Louis, and I was doing hair, but we were still pathetically poor. We could afford only a little two-room apartment. Even though we were struggling financially, I wanted children right away. I knew Larry would be a great father, and I knew I would be a great mother.

Now, my parents never talked to me about sex. The only thing I knew was that if I "went all the way," I'd get pregnant. Well, after I got married, naturally, I went all the way, but I didn't get pregnant. Larry and I went all the way *a lot*, but still no pregnancy. After six months, I was convinced there was something wrong with me, and I went to see a gynecologist. I had never seen a doctor before and was scared to death. I didn't know a thing about anything, though I knew that the Vinegar Treatment wouldn't work this time around.

When I got to the doctor's office, the very nice nurse took me to the exam room, gave me two piles of tissue paper, and started explaining things to me. I was so scared and nervous that I didn't hear a thing she said except get to undressed and cover myself up. I unfolded the papers. One was a large rectangle and the other was weirdly shaped with a hole in it.

I thought, "Oh that's nice. How thoughtful. The one with the hole goes over your coochie." So, I got undressed, covered my shoulders like a shawl with one sheet and tried to keep the one with the hole centered over my coochie. I left my shoes on, a pair of chunky sandals, put my feet in the stirrups, and lay back. I was trying desperately to keep myself covered with these tissue-thin sheets, and it was a real struggle.

Finally, the door opened and the doctor walked in. He took one look at me, lowered his eyes, and backed slowly out of the room. He was gone for ten minutes. All the while I struggled frantically to keep the paper in place. Then he came back in and, very politely, with the faintest little smile on his face, performed the examination through the little hole.

When he finished, he told me to sit up, but I couldn't because the straps of my sandals had gotten caught in the stirrups. The paper was sliding everywhere, and I was struggling to get my straps unstuck and still stay covered. It was ridiculous.

Once I was safely out of the stirrups and sitting up, the doctor told me that everything was fine. He patiently explained ovulation to me and told me when we should be having sex to conceive.

At my next visit, the nurse explained that the hole in the first sheet was for my head, not my coochie, and she showed me how to put everything on and cover myself properly. I'm certain that the first time I saw the doctor and he backed out of the room, he was trying desperately not to laugh and had to take time to compose himself. That's how naive I was about sex, pregnancy, doctor's offices, everything.

Once Larry and I knew what we were doing, I got pregnant right away. I had two miscarriages, but the third time was a charm. I delivered my first daughter, Diana, in 1968. My doctor never charged me a penny until she was delivered because he knew we didn't have any money or insurance. He was a doll, that doctor. Three years later, in 1971, I had my second daughter, Laura.

We were young, with two precious babies, and blissfully happy. But we still didn't have any money. Larry was working, but he didn't make much. By this time, I had given up working full time in the beauty salon, convinced that working there had caused my miscarriages. I also found it hard to work for other people. I always thought I could do what they were doing, only better.

I did the occasional head of hair, and I cleaned houses while my mother watched the girls. One day I heard from another beautician that mortuaries were paying as much as $100 a head for a hair style on the deceased. One hundred dollars! That was a fortune. I visited every funeral parlor in town until one hired me.

You know the old saying, be careful what you wish for? Well, when the day came for my first client, I was terrified. I enlisted my best friend, Maureen, to go with me.

Now, in 1972, there was no such thing as a blowout, so I had to wash and then manually roll the hair of the deceased in rollers, adjust the hair dryer, wait for the hair to dry, and then back-comb and style the hair. The whole process took about an hour and a half. The problem was, I couldn't bring myself to look at the dead person's face, so when I finished, my deceased client's hair was somewhat lopsided. But with coaching from Maureen and lots of hairspray, we made her beautiful. The mortician loved it, I was hired, and I had a new career.

Eventually, I could look at the faces and be alone with the bodies. I loved that job. The money was great, the hours were terrific—I could do a few heads a week and make great money—and I started to really enjoy it. But God had other plans for me. There was a young mortician there, a nephew of the owner, who was constantly trying to get my attention. I made it perfectly clear that I was happily married but he was a pest. Whenever I was in the basement working, he'd come down and stand as close to me as possible. He gave me the creeps, and I hated to be around him.

One day while I was working on a head of hair, he came downstairs and stood next to me. He kept inching closer and closer to me, and I kept inching away from him. But he just kept coming closer and closer. Before I knew it, he was chasing me around the table, with the dead body between us. I finally got away from him and fled upstairs. I was furious. I thought, "I have two little babies at home, and now I have to quit this good job because of this jerk. Now what am I going to do?"

Back then, sexual harassment was a routine part of a working woman's lot. But I knew his uncle would be very upset, so I ran upstairs and waited outside his uncle's office. A few minutes later, two men came out of the office in painter's clothes. I asked who the men were.

"They're painters," the mortician said. "They're going to paint the mortuary."

I said, "Really? What are they charging?"

He said, "$3,000," and, without thinking, I said, "I'll do it for $2,000."

The mortician looked at me, shocked, and said. "Really?" He thought for a minute, then said, "OK, you have yourself a deal."

I had no business experience, but something just clicked right then and there. It was divine inspiration. I was so furious about the position his nephew had put me in, so mad that I wasn't the captain of my own ship and that my life and work could be upended so easily by someone else. The words just came out, and I was in business for myself.

I had no idea what I was doing, business-wise, but I sure knew how to work hard, and I knew how to paint. By this time in my life, I had probably lived in a dozen places. Every time we rented a place, we cleaned it and painted or wallpapered it. We learned to do everything ourselves — painting, wallpapering, decorating, light construction, you name it. I knew a thing or two about painting and fixing up houses, so I wasn't worried about making good on my promise.

Diana and Laura were still very little, and Larry was working, so I hired my mother to paint the mortuary with me. We got the job done in a week, and the place looked great. The mortician was very pleased and promised to tell his friends. And I cleared almost $1,000 on the job. A thousand dollars! I had never seen so much money in my life. I was thrilled, Larry was thrilled, and I knew this was a road I was going to take.

After that, I opened up a painting and decorating business called A Woman's Touch. I was my own boss. I called the shots.

———

A Woman's Touch was very successful. My hook was that I hired only women — women who wanted to work part time, mothers who wanted out of the house or needed a little extra money. A woman-owned painting business was unusual at the time and still pretty rare today. This was (and probably still is) a trade usually reserved for men. I had no business background, but I knew how to work hard and get things done. I had common sense and street smarts, I wasn't shy, and I had an innate flair for marketing myself. I went to Brod Dugan Paints, then the biggest paint store in Saint Louis, and introduced myself.

I said, "We're a woman-owned business. We hire only women. We're neat, clean, and reliable, and we're bonded. We're going to be the best in Saint Louis. I'll buy all my paint and supplies here and only here, and if you have anybody who needs a painter, please recommend us."

I think they were tickled by my boldness and the novelty of my company, and they started recommending us. We got so much work that soon there was a months-long waiting list for our services. Within five years, we were the best painters in Saint Louis. It was pioneering, a woman-owned and -staffed painting company. The women I had working for me were terrific. They were just like me—mothers with children at home who needed extra money. They could work as much as they wanted, and the hours were flexible so they could spend time with their families. It worked great for everyone.

The painting jobs were done during the day, when most women were home alone. It turned out that women were more comfortable having women working in their houses than men, so work snowballed for us. I was very professional, and I was great at talking to people and getting them to like me (always the new kid!), so it was easy to get people's attention. I went to all the contractors in Saint Louis and urged them to hire A Woman's Touch, and they did.

But what really set us apart is that we did what we said we were going to do, when we said we were going to do it, for the price we said it would cost. If we said we were going to be there, we were there. It really had nothing to do with money. It didn't matter how much we charged as long as we did what we said we were going to do. And we did. That's the simplest business model in the world and the secret to success: Do what you're supposed to do, and do it well. Period.

From the start, my dad's motto ran through my head: "Good, better, best. Never let it rest until the good is the better and the better is the best." That kept me moving forward, always. I was never satisfied with being good. I had to get better so that I could be the best. And A Woman's Touch was the best, most successful painting company in Saint Louis. I am so proud of that accomplishment. I went from being poor, defenseless, and subject to the whims of others to being my own boss, the owner of a successful company. And it never would have happened if that jerk hadn't chased me around a dead body.

Dorothy, ca. 1944

Oscar and Dorothy, ca. 1944

Me, 1947

*Diane, me, Dorothy,
Oscar, and Randy, 1949*

Me, 1949

Diane, John, Dorothy, me, and Randy, 1951

My brother John, cousin Paul, and me

First grade, 1953

SCHOOL DAYS 1953-54
ADOLPH MEYER

Diane's birthday, 1956

My mother's parents,
Susanna and Charlie
Milbourn, 1956.
I was named after
my grandmother.

Washington School Days
1956 - 1957

Fourth grade and already
a fashionista, 1956

Dorothy, me, Oscar,
and John, 1957

Me chaperoning my sister, Diane, on a date, 1958.

JULY 1960

Twelve years old and on my way to Chicago, alone, to meet my Aunt Ruth, 1960

My senior photo, 1965

My wedding day, 1966

New Year's Eve, 1972

The McCarthy family, 1973

Laura, age 3, and Diana, age 5, 1973

Diana, 5th grade, and Laura, 3rd grade

Me on a cruise, 1983

Chapter Three
A Resale Queen Is Born

I owned and operated A Woman's Touch for 18 years, from 1972 to 1990. A Woman's Touch did very well. It put my girls through private school and college. Through all of this, Larry always said, "Go ahead!" He was always my biggest fan and biggest supporter. I always said, Larry made a good living, but I made the living good!

I didn't just run the company; I did a lot of the work myself. Having grown up the way I had, I wasn't afraid to roll up my sleeves and get to work. I wasn't afraid to climb up and down ladders and scaffolding. I was a terrific painter and paperhanger, and I always did the wallpaper jobs myself. I loved it.

One weekend in August 1990, Diana, who was home from college, was helping me paint an apartment. We finished the job and headed home. As soon as we walked in the door, the phone rang. The news was terrible: my sister, Diane, and one of her four daughters had been killed when their car was hit by a train. Her husband had died the year before, making her the single parent of four girls. It was devastating.

She had three surviving daughters, ages 26, 20, and 18. The oldest two were married, but the youngest one, Johnette, came to live with us. She was the same age as Laura. From that moment on, another phase of my life began. All I wanted was to do right by these girls and my own daughters. All I wanted was to make their lives as comfortable, stable, and pleasant as possible. All I wanted was to be there for my family.

My sister's death changed me forever, emotionally and spiritually. Soon after, I closed A Woman's Touch. A year later, I embarked on an entirely new career.

With three young women to raise, I had a clothing situation on my hands. These girls liked clothes —trendy, expensive clothes —lots of them, and I could barely keep up. I had made very good money with A Woman's Touch, but as a thrifty person, I never paid retail, and I certainly wasn't about to start.

I grew up shopping thrift stores and rummage sales. I loved the hunt, just as my mother had. So with the challenge of clothing three girls, I got moving. I started shopping garage sales, rummage sales, tag sales, and thrift shops. I combed the classifieds, shopped in basements and backyards, drove up and down side streets looking for "Sale" signs.

Now, at this time, 1990, the quality of the thrift stores was pretty bad. Choices were very limited, and you had to really look to find good-quality items in decent places. One day I was in a thrift store in south Saint Louis and another customer told me about a great new store that she had been to.

"It's really clean and nice and fancy," she said. "It's a consignment store."

She explained that consignment was where a seller brought an item to the store, the store sold it on the seller's behalf, and then the store split the sale price with the seller.

My fellow shopper said the merchandise was better than I'd find in a thrift store, so I headed over.

The second I walked into that consignment store I said to myself, "Oh, my God. I would love to do this, and I know I can do it better." The store was crowded with so much merchandise it was impossible to know where to start. The clothes were carelessly hung on wire hangers, and there was no rhyme or reason to the racks. Pants, shirts, jackets, blouses, winter coats, and swimsuits were all jumbled together. It was a mess.

I knew I could do it better. It was just like when that car door opened and there was Larry, the man *I knew* I was going to marry. It was just like when the mortician told me he was going to pay $3,000 to have his place painted, and *I knew* I could do it better and cheaper.

When I walked into that consignment shop, I knew that my life would change. I knew that I could do consignment, that I could do it better, and that I would be the best at it.

I went right up to the counter, introduced myself to the owner, and told her the truth—that I was interested in the business and wanted to start my own. She graciously told me all about her business, how consignment worked, and offered me a job on the spot. I accepted and started work the following week.

I worked there only one day, and in that one day I learned everything wrong with her business and everything that I did *not* want to do. I understood numbers, supply and demand, and expenses, so the things I saw that day were astounding to me. First, the owner was a slave to her suppliers, the people whose clothes she was selling. Second, half of her store was given over to items that she was waiting to *return* to her suppliers. These were items that she couldn't sell at the agreed-upon price, and they were taking up a lot of valuable space. That's inventory control, and hers was way out of balance.

I said to her, "You've got 1,000 square feet here, and 500 of that is nothing but things going back to suppliers. Why don't you just get rid of this stuff? Sell it off quickly and cheaply and move it out?"

And she said, "Oh, I can't do that. What would they think of me?"

She was afraid to sell the merchandise for a lower price because she had promised her suppliers a certain price for their items, so she'd rather return it than disappoint them. So for those items (about half the store), no one made any money except the landlord. And the space that was taken up with items that *weren't* for sale prevented her from using it for items that *were* for sale.

The third mistake was that she allowed her suppliers to set the price. If someone came in with a shirt, she'd ask, "What do you want for it?" If they paid $20 for the shirt, they told her they wanted $15, and that's the price she would set. That's crazy. You can't sell a used item for the retail price. She should have sold the shirt for $8-$10 and split the money with the supplier. And because she was afraid to mark merchandise down, it sat there, taking up valuable space.

Like many businesses, resale is based on price points and volume. Consumers are savvy. They know what a shirt from the Gap retails for, and they have an instinct for what they should pay for a used item. The bottom line is that an item is only worth what you are able to sell it for. If it isn't priced right, it won't move; and if it won't move, you won't make any money,

You have to find the sweet spot, that price point where a consumer will buy an item and where you can make money. To this day, I still tell my suppliers there is a fine line between making them happy and making a profit.

In consignment, you pretty much make money only on volume, because you are splitting the sale price with the owner of the item. And from your portion, you pay all the expenses—rent, insurance, utilities, advertising, and payroll—and take all the risks, so you need to move a lot of merchandise to make money.

But this shop owner wasn't doing that. Her prices were too high, so she was sitting on piles of merchandise that she couldn't sell. It appeared that she was losing money pretty quickly. And she couldn't afford to put any work or effort into the store's appearance. She was spending more time and effort returning merchandise to her suppliers than selling it.

The fourth big mistake was that the shop was dark, dirty, and uninviting, and the clothes were not organized by color or type or size or season or any familiar system. And the quality of the clothes wasn't good. Because she couldn't say no to anyone, she took everything that came in: items that weren't sellable; items of poor quality; items that were out of style; and items with missing buttons, ripped hems, stains, and scuff marks. You can't sell a shirt with a big stain on it or a jacket that's missing buttons or a skirt with a ripped hem no matter what the label is. There were some decent items in the store, but the place was so disorganized and overpacked with merchandise that even the good stuff was buried.

I learned on that first day not to let the suppliers call the shots and run the business. I knew I couldn't do a good job if

I didn't manage their expectations and set my own prices, realistic ones. The suppliers would have to be educated and managed properly if anyone was going to make money. The shop had to be organized, nicely lighted, well furnished, and welcoming. The clothes had to be high quality, ready to wear, and organized by size, style, and season. I saw immediately the way I'd run a consignment business and how I would make a profit.

At the end of my first, and last, day of work, I went home and told Larry what I wanted to do: open my own consignment store. As always, he said, "Great! Do it!" He knew I could do it. Once again, my business model was, "Tell people what you're going to do, and do it right."

I immediately set out looking for my own space. Of course, once again, my dad's motto was running through my head: "Good, better, best. Never let it rest until the good is the better and the better is the best." And I had to be the best. Like A Woman's Touch, whatever I did had to be done better than anyone else, and I knew that I could nail the consignment business. And I did. When I opened my first store, there were about twenty other consignment stores in Saint Louis. Every one of them is closed now.

I quickly found a little 400 square-foot space on Mackenzie and Gravois. I called it Women's Closet Exchange and opened in the spring of 1991. I chose the name because I thought it evoked what we did—exchange items from women's closets. (Two years later, I regretted the name, thinking it was too long.) It was a good location, on a busy road with high visibility at a rent I could afford. The only problem was that I had no clothes to sell. I went home and took everything out of my closet and the girls' closets, and I put it in the store. I had five racks. I put three racks in the front of the store and filled them with well-organized, color-coordinated merchandise. I filled the other two racks with merchandise and put those in the back room.

I cracked open the door to the back room about six inches or so and positioned those extra racks so that all you could see were racks of clothes. It was just a little peek, but it looked like the back room was full. When people walked in, I said, "Thank you for coming. We have all kinds of stuff in the back room, too, that we've just gotten in and are processing. So every time you come in, it's a whole new store!" I wanted to give the impression of abundance, of more, more, more, and that you'd have to keep coming back to see the new stuff. (I am a big fan of the adage, "Fake it 'til you make it.") It was enticing, and it worked. If you don't find something today, you've got to come back.

From the start, I did things differently. First, my store was bright and clean and welcoming. Second, I took my display areas seriously. Third, I did what the department stores do—put only seasonal or preseasonal merchandise on the floor. That means winter coats started to appear in September and spring dresses came out in February. Fourth, and most important, I called the shots with the sellers. I told them what items I wanted to sell and what price I could sell them for, rather than letting them tell me what they wanted. I graciously refused items that were not up to my standards or that were not seasonal or stylish. That is the key to success in consignment.

For example, if a woman came in with a blazer, I told her the price I could sell it for. The seller would get 50 percent of the sale price. If the item didn't sell at the initial price within thirty days, the item would be marked down until it sold, and their percentage of the sale price would stay the same, fifty percent. If after sixty days an item didn't sell, it would be donated. I did not return items under $50. Those were the terms, and I stuck to my guns.

The only way I could make money was to be in complete control of the sale price and complete control of the inventory, which had to be moved quickly to make money. I had to educate my suppliers about the way the business worked. If they didn't like the price I was offering, they had every right to walk away, no hard feelings. I always strove to be realistic about pricing and to be fair to my suppliers.

I was and still am always incredibly polite and generous with my suppliers. If I don't have suppliers I don't have merchandise to sell. And I want them to keep coming back with merchandise. But this is a two-way street—I can't sell their merchandise and make a profit if the sale price is unreasonable and if I don't have the flexibility to mark items down and move them out. There was a lot of education for everyone in those early days.

I also took only good-quality items that were in good condition. If an item was good quality but dated, I didn't take it. If heels were too scuffed or handbags too worn, I didn't take them. I wanted to sell items that were current, well made, well maintained, and ready to wear, meaning no loose buttons or hems. Back then, I remember turning down vintage Louis Vuitton—the few times I took it I couldn't give it away. People simply weren't familiar with the brand. (Those were the days...)

I ran a tight ship. I was firm with my suppliers but always fair and friendly. Word quickly got out, and I soon had an enormous roster of suppliers. I also quickly outgrew my space, so I expanded into the space next door, adding another 400 square feet. That soon became too small as well.

After the first two years, I found a darling little house in an affluent neighborhood called Sunset Hills. We fixed it up, and it was absolutely charming. Business was booming. I kept getting bigger and better every year. Before I knew it, I had three locations. I wanted to be the best, and by 2000 I was.

I made a lot of mistakes, though. When I first started, I advertised everywhere — in newspapers, in restaurants, on shopping carts, wherever a sales rep talked me into advertising. Talk about a thousand mistakes. But I quickly learned that the very best advertising is word of mouth. If you do a good job, people will talk about it. They will tell their friends, who will come in to see for themselves; and then they will tell their friends, who will come in, and so on. If you do what you say you're going to do and do it better than anyone else, the business will come. Keep your promises, be fair and honest, and always do the right thing. That's the best way to run a business and live your life.

For the first twenty years we were in business, we were strictly consignment. That was really the only business model out there. It's what most stores did. And as a business model, it made sense if you were just starting out. With consignment, you don't have to buy inventory. You have to secure a space and maintain it, but overhead is relatively low because you don't have to purchase any merchandise.

But consignment has a few major downsides. First, you have to sell a lot of inventory to make money, so you have to have a lot of inventory always coming in. Second, the accounting is exhausting. Every item has to be processed and logged and kept track of meticulously, and every seller has to have a file and a code. Say Susan Smith brings in a blouse. You say you will sell it for $20, and she will get forty percent of the sale price. When the item sells, you have to record how much the item went for and how much is due to the seller so you can cut her a check at the end of the month. Simple, right? Yes, but when you have thousands of items from hundreds or thousands of suppliers across two or three stores, it becomes a real pain.

You often spend more time on the logistics and accounting behind the sale than anything else. It gets complicated pretty fast. (To be fair, I was doing consignment before reliable customer-service software was affordable for small shops like mine, so we had to do everything by hand.) Plus, you have to field calls from anxious suppliers, calling to ask if their items have sold. And a supplier can always come in and request her item back. That was a real nightmare. We had to search through the racks until we found it, and we might have moved the item to another store.

Consignment was great, but it always bothered me for those reasons. It seemed excessively complicated. I knew there had to be an easier, better way.

As in everything I did, I took my business seriously. I wanted to be the best, and I was constantly trying out new things, getting ideas from anywhere I could. To be successful, you have to change and grow and be open to new ideas. And you should never think you know everything. You have to learn what works and what doesn't, try new things, and shift your perspective. I talked to professionals in retail, sales, marketing, and other professions to learn as much as I could about business and sales. I joined local and national trade associations and went to annual conferences to meet other resale professionals. I was constantly trying to educate myself to make my business better.

In 2004, I was at the annual conference of the National Association of Resale Professionals (NARTS). There, I met and spent time with Spencer and Kristen Block, the owners of a national resale chain called Buffalo Exchange. Spencer and Kristen were experts at buying inventory outright, and Buffalo Exchange was very successful. They were lovely, open, and generous people, and they explained their business model to me. After meeting them, I was convinced that their business model could work for me.

I returned to Saint Louis and decided to try buying merchandise outright. When suppliers came in, I offered two options: I could consign the item and they would get fifty percent of the sale price (which was not guaranteed because the item might get marked down or not sell at all), or I could buy the item outright from them. The buyout price was usually somewhat lower than what they might have gotten at the consignment price, but with the buyout they could leave right then and there with cash in hand.

Immediately, ninety-five percent of my suppliers chose the buyout option. Payment on the spot was key. They could wait and potentially get a higher price, but there was no guarantee that the item would sell for that initial price—or sell at all—so they had incentive to sell right away. I learned very quickly that most people just wanted to be rid of their stuff.

Within a year I phased out consignment and moved entirely to the buyout model. To make a profit with the buyout model, I had to take into consideration many factors. The most important was that not every item is going to sell for the initial sale price. Given the vagaries of fashion and the whims of buyers, about twenty-five percent of items end up being marked down. I had to create some wiggle room for myself, which meant I had to again educate my suppliers.

The other innovation I learned was to offer store credit to my suppliers. I would offer a set price for cash and then a slightly higher price in store credit. This kept suppliers in my store as both buyers *and* sellers, and invariably ensured repeat business. About half of my suppliers take the store credit option today.

The new model worked brilliantly. I knew there had to be a better way, and I just kept myself open to finding out what it was. People get in trouble when they think they know everything. I encounter that a lot in my business. Actually, I encounter that a lot in *all* businesses. Never think you've got it all figured out, that there's no room for improvement, or that you can't learn anything new.

When I go to our national conferences now, I talk to as many people as I can. At this point in my resale career— twenty-six years, seven stores, and many millions in resale dollars under my belt—I am considered a leader in the industry. But I always seek out young people and people new to the industry to hear what they are doing, because I know I can learn something from them. I learn more from them than they learn from me. They're looking at it from a new perspective, and a new perspective is always fresh and clean.

If you want to be the best, listen and learn from others. The minute you think you know everything, you are doomed. You have to innovate, grow, and change. And listen to what your customers tell you. Customers are royalty, especially the ones with closets full of Manolo Blahniks.

Why we hate fakes, and why we authenticate

We hate fakes, by which we mean knockoffs. We love fashion, and we have deep appreciation and respect for the artistry, craftsmanship, and design that go into making luxury items. To steal from a designer, maker, or artist is wrong. It's illegal and unethical. Furthermore, the counterfeit market is rife with criminal activity and unfair and disturbing labor practices, like child and slave labor. You might think that the Louis Vuitton or Kate Spade handbag you buy on the street for $35 is a harmless purchase, but the fact is that you are supporting a criminal network that both harms the integrity of the original maker and supports illegal labor practices.

We will not buy fakes, and we authenticate every item before it hits our floor. We stand by everything we sell as 100 percent authentic.

Chapter Four

The Chicago Buy — A Blizzard of Blahniks

Today, the Vault Luxury Resale is a leader in the luxury resale industry. With labels like Chanel, Gucci, Hermès, Prada, Kate Spade, and Tory Burch, we attract some of the best suppliers and customers in the country.

But when we started out, the biggest name we sold was probably Ann Taylor. The items we carried were good quality, clean, and current, but we weren't a high-end designer resale shop. We sold the occasional piece from Calvin Klein or Diane von Furstenberg, maybe an occasional Hermès scarf or Gucci belt, but the majority of our labels were specialty and department store brands, popular items from popular brands for the everyday woman.

In 2005, everything changed. I had just completed the switch from consignment to buyout, and business was booming. People came from all over the Saint Louis area and beyond to sell us their items and buy our merchandise. I had the pick of the litter, as it were, and chose only the best items that came in. People knew they could get cash on the spot with no hassle, so word spread, and we were very busy.

I was increasingly the face of resale and was serving as the vice president of the National Association of Resale

Professionals. I was traveling the country consulting and speaking at conferences about resale and how we did business. We now had a national presence because of my speaking engagements, the Internet, and the incredible word of mouth about our business.

One day in May of 2005, I got a phone call from a man in Chicago who had heard about us from a local news story. He said his mother had recently passed away and wondered if I would be willing to come to Chicago to look at some of her things. He said his mother had closets full of designer items, and he wanted us to help him with the removal of her things.

Now, we were sometimes called by agents and dealers in Saint Louis to be the first at estate sales to look at the clothing and accessories, but the clothing was usually older than what we could use, so I was a little skeptical about this one, too. We did not do vintage. But he described some of the items his mother had. He said some very big names — Hermès, Prada, Chanel. We had a few of those items in our stores, but not many. He kept repeating that he had hundreds of items and wanted to get rid of everything.

I told him to send me a few pictures and I would get back to him. I remember thinking, "Drive all the way to Chicago to look at his mother's clothes? Why would I do that? That's crazy!"

The next day, he emailed me a dozen pictures of very high-quality items. He included his address in Chicago, which I recognized as a very wealthy area. Based on what I saw, and a little spidey sense, I decided to go for it. The voice in my head told me to do it, but my daughters and my staff thought I was nuts. But my mind was made up. I told everyone exactly where I was going and whom I was going to meet, and I said that if I didn't call to check in by noon to send the police.

The next morning, I left Saint Louis at 5 a.m. and headed north for the five-hour drive to Chicago. I was intrigued and confident about what I was about to do, but I'd be lying if I said I wasn't a teeny bit nervous, too. At least three times on the way, I seriously considered turning around. But my gut told me this was the right thing to do.

I arrived in the Chicago suburb about 10 a.m. This was one of the most affluent areas of the country, and the house looked about as old money as you can get—stately and massive. I pulled up, parked, walked to the front door, and rang the bell. A housekeeper ushered me in and went off to find "Mr. John." I waited in the foyer and took everything in: marble and dark polished wood, an ornate antique round walnut table on which drooped beautiful calla lilies, an enormous highly polished curved staircase leading to I had no idea how many floors above.

Then I heard the yapping of dogs, and the son approached. Mid-sixties I guessed, rumpled but conservatively stylish: Ralph Lauren shirt and trousers, Gucci loafers, three yappy Yorkies at his heels.

"You must be Sue," he said, offering his hand. "Thank you so much for making the journey. I hope it is worth your while. Mother would have been so pleased to see you. Please follow me."

He led me though the house, which was huge and absolutely spotless. Every surface and floor gleamed with polish. The house was very tasteful and well decorated, but it was dated. It looked as if nothing had been touched or altered in thirty years. It was also as quiet as a mausoleum. The only sounds were our footsteps, the son's soft voice, and the clicking of the little Yorkies' toenails on the marble floors.

As we approached the back of the house, he talked quietly about "Mother"—how old she was when she passed away (eighty-seven), how she had lived alone except for her live-in staff since his father died twenty years ago, how she loved fashion and followed all the trends. Mother this and Mother that. I have to say, he was starting to creep me out a little. In my mind, I dubbed him Norman Bates, after the creepy son in *Psycho*. I started to get a little nervous. I thought to myself, "Great job, Sue. This guy's going to kill you and stuff you and put you in a chair next to 'Mother' and the dogs."

But treasure hunter that I am, I pressed on and followed Norman to the back of the house, where he said Mother's main closet was kept. "Mother was quite a fashionista," he said.

Looking around the dated 1970s décor, I started to have some serious doubts. What if he had just sent me pictures from the Internet of Chanel bags and Hermès scarves? What kind of prize idiot was I? Driving five hours to a complete stranger's house to look at handbags and clothes? *What was I thinking?*

He paused outside a huge wooden door and said, "Here we are."

As he opened the door, I was sure I would find his mother in a rocking chair, stuffed and lifeless, but when he switched on the light, the "Hallelujah" chorus began to play in my head. An entire wall was just handbags, dozens of beautiful, mint-condition designer handbags, each of which had been lovingly given its own little shelf. I immediately recognized Chanel, Dior, Louis Vuitton, and Hermès. Absolutely gorgeous bags.

I stepped into the room. On the adjacent wall were racks of gorgeous blouses, skirts, and suits. Chanel, Yves Saint Laurent, Calvin Klein, and Armani. My eyes were bugging out of my head. I was speechless. My head was spinning. I was, quite literally, taken aback. As I stepped back to take it all in, I backed right into another wall, a wall of nothing but shoes. I was so flummoxed that I tripped on the carpet, crashed into the shelves, and fell to the floor. The shelves of shoes crashed down on top of me. I was covered in Manolo Blahniks, Jimmy Choos, and Stuart Weitzmans. I was swimming in a sea of shoes.

"Oh dear," said Norman. "Are you all right?"

I was more than all right. I was in heaven. I was picking up each shoe and looking at it like I was in *Raiders of the Lost Ark*. I'd found the treasure! I was so excited I could barely contain myself, but at the same time I was trying desperately to maintain a poker face, because you never want to be too excited in front of a supplier. But inside I was *dying*. I had never seen anything like it.

Despite the dated decor, the items in that closet were all beautiful and current and the height of fashion. Norman's mother obviously had a huge shopping problem. Most of the items still had the price tags on them. All the shoes were in boxes. This woman was an avid reader of *Women's Wear Daily*, *Vogue*, and *Harper's Bazaar*. She knew what was fashionable, and she bought only the best labels. Norman told me she would see something she liked in a magazine and then order it from Neiman Marcus, Barney's, Saks Fifth Avenue, or right from the designer. When the item arrived, she would tear the page out of the magazine and slip the page into the shoebox or the purse or the jacket pocket. She was a collector.

But that wasn't all. Norman said, "This is only one of her closets. She had two more."

Two more? Be still my heart! I followed him upstairs where he showed me two huge walk-in closets, both chock full of gorgeous designer items. It was unreal. These items were somewhat older but still gorgeous and in fabulous condition.

I excused myself and left to call the store. I said, "Not only am I safe, but this is the mother lode. This is incredible. Get two vans and drive up here now."

I returned to Norman and asked him what he was interested in getting rid of. "Absolutely everything," he said. "I want everything gone. I don't want to keep a thing." I told him I needed some time to work up an estimate, and he said, "Take your time, dear lady, take your time," and disappeared with the Yorkies downstairs.

I spent the next several hours taking notes, cataloging and categorizing, running up and down the stairs, trying to come up with a figure. The clothes and accessories were divine, absolutely the best quality. But I knew I was going to be able to sell only about half of what was there and that I would have to get rid of the other half, so I had to take that into consideration.

This was the first time I had ever bought in such bulk. Up to then, we'd probably never bought more than fifty items at once. Here I was looking at *hundreds* of items. I really had to think things through.

Finally, I had some idea of what I could sell the items for

and what I was willing to pay. It was time to negotiate with Norman. The maid was waiting for me at the bottom of the stairs, and she led me to a wood-paneled study where Norman was having tea with the Yorkies and reading *The Wall Street Journal*. It was May but there was a fire blazing in the fireplace.

I thanked him for inviting me and offering me the opportunity to look at his mother's things. I explained that though everything was lovely, I could sell only sell part of her collection. I told him I would take everything though, pay him for the items that I wanted, arrange for the donation of the rest, and see that he got the proper tax receipts for the donation. I asked him if he had a price in mind.

He said, "Whatever you think. I just want everything gone. I want to get rid of everything. How about a few thousand?" A figure popped into my head; I offered it, and he accepted and said he was thrilled.

I gave Norman a check on the spot. He shook my hand and thanked me. He said the maid would help me in whatever way I needed, and he left. I started packing everything up and waited for the girls to arrive from Saint Louis to help me. They arrived about 7 p.m., and we loaded everything into the two vans and my car. The vehicles were so packed and overloaded, you couldn't see out of the windows. It's a wonder we didn't crash on the way back to Saint Louis. Death by dresses. What a way to go!

We got back to Saint Louis well after midnight. After a good night's rest, we cleared out an entire room for the items. Before the Chicago Haul (as we came to call this buyout), we sold the occasional Chanel bag, Hermès scarf, and pair of

Manolo Blahniks, but those labels were not our usual brands. Now we had hundreds of these items to process and put out on the floor. We had to do a lot of research in order to set prices. It took us weeks to process the items, and the entire staff worked together on the haul.

When everything was ready, I called a friend of mine at the *St. Louis Post-Dispatch* and told her about our haul, that we had lots of Chanel and Gucci handbags, thirty pairs of Manolo Blahniks, and dozens of other designer items. She did a little story on us. A local TV station picked it up and sent a crew to do a story on us, too.

Once those stories hit, word got out and there was a line out the door. We sold those items so quickly our heads spun. Ultimately, that buyout, coupled with our many weeks of hard work, due diligence, research, and investment, netted us a tremendous profit and great publicity. And it opened a door, ushering in a new way for us to do business—the closet buy. I am very, very grateful to Norman and his mother's closet.

From that first closet buy, we became the queens of up-scale resale. Now we were the only place to go to buy and sell luxury designer goods. Suddenly, we were flooded with Louis Vuitton, Gucci, Dior, Hermès, and more. People who never would have dreamed of shopping resale or selling their items were suddenly our biggest and best clients. The brands we started taking in shifted. We still took high-quality de-partment store and boutique brands like J. Crew, Banana Republic, Coach, Ann Taylor, Loft, and the like, but now we also took Louis Vuitton, Manolo Blahnik, Chanel, Prada, Gucci, and others.

We were so successful that year that I took my entire staff on a Caribbean cruise for Christmas. The Chicago Haul was the Mother of All Closets. It's still one of the biggest and most lucrative closet buys we've ever done. But it certainly wasn't the strangest. No, that would be the Hot Mess in New York. Or maybe the escorts in Vegas. Or the mistress in Paris. Well, you can decide.

Chapter Five
A Family Affair

The Vault Luxury Resale is a family business. My daughters Diana and Laura work with me every day. They fell in love with the business just like I did. They joined me and never looked back.

Laura was the first to join. In 1998, she was taking college classes and working as a waitress. She was considering a career in theater and voice work and was taking classes at a local performing arts school as well. Instead of waiting tables, I told her to come work for me, where she could make more money and have a better schedule to take classes and study.

She came to work at WCE and loved it right away. She was young and fashionable, and I think she was impressed with the caliber of the items we had in the store. Suddenly it didn't seem like her mom's business anymore; it was cool and hip. She saw that I wasn't selling used clothing; I was selling luxury, fashion, and style. And I could see that she was a great and immediate fit for the business.

Laura is a label savant. She has a knack for fashion and style, and she is so authentic in her approach that people just flocked to her for style advice. She was a great salesperson not because she could sell, but because she was honest about what looked good on someone. People trusted her. Plus, she became the store's best buyer almost immediately. She knew what was hot, what was classic, what was trendy. She knew what women wanted or would want. She knew what was lovely but wouldn't sell. She was a natural at resale.

After a year, Laura was hooked—so hooked, in fact, that she quit school and came to work with me full time. A few years later she wanted to branch out and start her own store—an upscale resale shop selling maternity, baby, and children's clothing and accessories. Laura had just gotten married and she had no kids of her own. I didn't think she knew anything about maternity or children's clothing, so I was skeptical that it would succeed. Upscale kids' stuff? I didn't think it would fly.

But Laura dealt directly with our customers. She knew them and their buying habits intimately, and she knew that many of them had children. She knew that the type of woman who buys or sells a Coach or Tory Burch bag might also buy a Bodin or Lilly Pulitzer dress for her daughter or little Ralph Lauren Polo shirts and Northface jackets for her son, not to mention the accessories—chic Kate Spade diaper bags, Bugaboo strollers, Hunter boots. Laura knew that when your child grows out of something, it's just taking up real estate. If the moms were already motivated to bring us their items, why wouldn't they bring us their kids' items as well? And if a customer who liked to shop resale had kids or was expecting, why wouldn't she patronize a resale shop that catered to their little ones? Laura knew there was a market there, and she wanted to act on it.

So, in 2001, Laura rented a space next door to Women's Closet Exchange and opened Purple Cow Kids. It was the first upscale resale boutique in St. Louis for children's clothing and accessories, and it took off immediately. The customers loved it. Women could now come to WCE to buy and sell their items, and then pop next door to buy and sell items for their children. It was terrific. Home run for Laura! I was so proud of her. Her idea was great and she nailed it. The children's store was such a success that three years later, she opened a teen boutique called Clique right next to the Purple Cow. Now we covered every age group!

—⟨⟩ ⟨⟩—

At the same time, my older daughter Diana, armed with a degree in marketing and communications from Saint Louis University, was working as conference director at Maritz Travel, where she planned and managed corporate and private conferences and luxury incentive travel for Fortune 500 companies. She had been a concierge at the Ritz, so she knew how to deliver for her clients. She had traveled to and planned events on all seven continents, including Antarctica. She loved what she did, and she was very good at it: In 1999, she won an ILEA Award from the International Live Event Association for planning the year's best event—in this case a spectacular wedding with a budget of $500,000. Diana knew the world of luxury. She knew, better than any of us, how to deliver a luxurious, high-end experience. That's what she did for a living, and she was one of the best in the business.

In 2009, after she had her second child, Diana wanted to slow down a bit. She loved the travel and the planning, but it became grueling. She saw how much Laura and I were enjoying working together, and I suggested she do something with us. So, Diana started the Shopping Company, which offered luxury shopping tours in Saint Louis and excursions to New York, Chicago, Scottsdale, London, and Paris that featured insider access to the best in shopping, dining, and nightlife. She marketed it to our customers and led the tours, and I went along on the trips. Our customers loved it.

Diana quit Maritz and came to work with us full-time. She continued offering and running the tours (which are now offered under the Vault's name) and also took on our PR, marketing, promotions, and special events. Diana really took our company to new places, and we started getting incredible press. She organized new special events like runway shows, Wine Wednesdays, Sunday teas, Handbag Extravaganzas, VIP events, and more. I saw immediately that having Diana on board completed the company. She became our partner. The girls and I made a great team and working together every day was—and is—a real joy.

A lot of people can't believe that a mother and her two daughters can work well together, but we do. I'm passionate about resale, customer service, and what I do. When the girls started working with me, they became as passionate as me, and immediately relished their roles in the business.

I love working with my daughters, and since they joined the team, our revenues have doubled. Now, we certainly have our issues. What family doesn't? But because we each have different talents that we bring to bear on the specific things we are responsible for in our company, we rarely step on each other's toes or cause hard feelings. And when we do, we may fight and yell and scream and cry, but we get over it very quickly and it's always resolved in a day. There's never any jealousy or hard feelings.

Not only do we work together every day, we live within a few miles of each other, and we vacation together—all three families—three times a year. Diana's and Laura's kids are the same ages. We see each other every day, no matter what. Is it unusual that we work together and vacation together and love being with each other every day? Maybe, but it's the way we live and work, and we love it.

I think what makes it work so well is that we respect each other and the talents that we each have. We all love fashion and luxury items and travel, but we each bring a little something different to the table. I have an innate business sense that helps me choose great locations for stores. I have a natural curiosity (and small ego) that helps me learn from likely and unlikely places. I am the CEO, and I now take a much more expansive view of the business, allowing my daughters to take the lead on a day-to-day basis. My trust in them is complete, as is my appreciation of their strengths.

Laura has a great eye, is very well educated on labels, and knows who the upcoming designers are. She knows instinctively what will sell now and in a few months. And she knows what won't sell, which is as important. She knows what not to buy, so we don't get inundated with merchandise that won't sell. That's really the most important aspect of the business: buying the right items, at the right price, that will sell. Her thinking is, "What are we going to sell it for?" She'll pass on things that the rest of us would jump at.

I'll say, "Laura, that was Armani!" And she'll say, "I know, Mom, but it was from 1980, and we'll never sell it. If we do sell it, we're not going to sell it for much. Do we want to invest our money in that? No. We want to wait for a sure-sell." And she's always right! Just because we think something is fabulous doesn't mean it will sell, and Laura knows that better than anyone. She's not blinded by labels. She also coined our mantra, "Beware of items with price tags."

Laura's a savvy investor of our money. She knows what to buy and the price to pay for it so that we make money and make our clients happy. And she's incredible at sales. If something doesn't look good on you, she'll steer you to something more flattering. She'd rather not make a sale than sell you something you won't wear or doesn't look good.

Diana knows luxury, knows how people want to be treated, and knows marketing. The events and marketing she has done for us have skyrocketed us into the upper echelon of Saint Louis society. We sit at the front table of most social events because of her. Her efforts have led to our position as one of the finest upscale resale shops in the country.

We get the closet buys we do because of Diana's marketing. She knows how to position us in front of the right people at the right time. Her events are lavish and fun, as well as profitable. She got us involved in wonderful industry events like Fashion Week and the Saint Louis Fashion Fund. We are dealing with the top people in the country who meet our criteria for what they want to sell, and that's all because of Diana. She's the one who executes our vision. She's the one who makes sure the champagne is chilled, the gift bags are filled, the couches are fluffed, and the doors are opened on time. Her events are fabulous, and she markets and executes them with an eye to detail that is remarkable.

Diana also found a way for us to give back by hosting charity events at the Vault. We pay for everything—food, drinks, valet, staffing—and then donate a portion of our sales to the cause. We host dozens throughout the year, and Diana organizes every one of them. It's a wonderful way for us to give back to our customers and community.

Once my girls joined the team, it freed me up to do more traveling, which I love. Wherever I am, I try to incorporate a closet buy if I can. Wherever I go, I pop into stores and boutiques—both new and resale—to see how other people are doing things, how items are organized and displayed, and how customers are treated. I always learn new things wherever I go, and having the girls working with me, knowing that my business is in really good hands, enables me to explore a bit more.

Our lives are blessed. And believe me, I know how fortunate I am to have my daughters with me every day, doing what we love.

Chapter Six
French Kiss — The Paris Buys

hanks to our 2013 reality show on the Style Network, *Resale Royalty*, the Vault Luxury Resale is known around the world, and we have FedEx boxes arriving daily from all around the country, plus South America, China, and Europe. Our Internet footprint is pretty big these days, and we do a lot of business internationally. But in the mid-2000s, most of our buying and selling was based on word of mouth—one happy client or supplier would tell another, who would tell another, who would tell another, and the ball just rolled merrily along.

One day, back in 2008, I got a call from a woman in France. Her name was Georgette, and she said she had heard about our store from friends in the US. She would be traveling to Saint Louis with her husband on business and wanted to stop in. She had heard that we carried current Hermès, Céline, Chanel, and other designers and was wondering if we could pull some things for her prior to her arrival. I said, "Absolutely." (As is the case with most of our international clients, Georgette spoke perfect English. The majority of our international clients are well educated and sophisticated, and they travel extensively.)

Georgette arrived two weeks later, and we opened the store an hour early so she could shop privately. Tall, slim, and impossibly beautiful, she possessed that *je ne sais quoi*, that simple elegance that all French women seem to be born with. She arrived in a Chloé coat, Yves Saint Laurent booties, Céline trousers and silk shirt, and, of course, an Hermès scarf tied perfectly around her neck. (How do French women do that?) Her hair was subtly highlighted, and she smelled faintly but deliciously of what we later learned was Iris Poudre by Frederic Malle.

We greeted her, led her to our sitting area, served her coffee and scones from our favorite local bakery (which, naturally, she did not eat), and showed her the items we had pulled for her: a dozen handbags, a few pieces of jewelry, an assortment of silk scarves, and a few lovely coats. She dismissed the coats and jewelry but fell in love with the bags. She chose two Chanel bags and a Fendi baguette. Then, she circled the store a few times, picking up a Gucci belt, a great pair of Rag & Bone boots, an Alexander McQueen scarf, and two David Yurman rings. She paid for her purchases and left very happy, on her way to meet her husband for brunch at the Four Seasons.

"Au revoir," she waved, and said she would be in touch.

A few months later, we got another call from Georgette. She said she was ready to part with some of her things, and would we be willing to come to Paris for the buy? Now, as enticing as a trip to Paris might be, we had to be sure it would be worth our time and expense. We are business people. We are not frivolous with our time and money. When we do closet buys, we always do our research first to make sure the seller has items that we can actually resell at a profit and enough items to make it worth our time and expense to travel there. We also need to be sure that there are items other than clothing. As much as we love clothing, we need to have handbags and jewelry in addition to clothes to make it profitable. And if we fly somewhere to do a buy, we suggest that the seller contact two or three of her friends so we can maximize our time and effort. So, we asked Georgette if she had any friends who might be interested. She said she would check and get back to me.

Diana did the vetting, and she made it perfectly clear what our criteria were for the items we were seeking. Georgette discussed in detail with Diana the items she was willing to part with—what the items were, where she had purchased them, what the retail prices were, the conditions, sizes, and so on. Diana also talked to two of Georgette's friends who wanted to sell some things. Diana determined that Georgette and her friends had lots of fabulous items they wanted to sell and, more important, that we would be able to resell for a profit. This trip could be well worth it, so we booked our flight to Paris.

Generally speaking, what people think they have and what they actually have, in terms of resale value, are two completely different things. Some people think because they paid $2,000 for a Prada jacket that we're going to fall over ourselves and automatically buy it from them, but they're wrong. First, the size may not work for the majority of our customers. Second, it may not be current or on trend, meaning it's out of style, too old for current sale, or not old enough to be vintage. Third, even if the item is current and desirable, we can give only a fraction of the purchase price because we are going to resell it for a fraction of the original retail price, and that's only if it is in excellent condition. Finally, and this is especially true for items owned by Europeans, the items might be too worn — or, as we like to say, "loved too much" — to resell.

Europeans tend to buy high-quality items, just a few, and then wear them well. So, by the time they are willing to part with an item, it shows too much wear to resell. Luckily for us, the US is a more throwaway society. We buy something, we wear it for a season, and then we want to get rid of it. Americans tend to have more current items that are lightly worn, if they are worn at all.

However, with Europeans, it's a generational thing. Our younger, very wealthy European clients tend to have much newer items, and they don't tend to keep them very long. Because they travel often, they are always buying new items, and they usually want to get rid of their things quickly so they can buy more. After all, even the richest people in the world have to deal with closet space.

We arrived in Paris on a crisp, beautiful October morning and went right to our favorite hotel, the Four Seasons George V. We'd slept on the flight, so we checked in, freshened up, and headed out.

We strolled down the Champs-Élysées, where we popped into the world's best stores — Louis Vuitton, Hermès, Chanel, Gucci, Céline, and Balenciaga, plus less expensive, trendy shops like H&M and Zara — to see what was new in the world of fashion and style. We had lunch at famed Parisian Café Les Deux Magots. After lunch, we hit the famous Paris open markets, where we always find great items and bargains for ourselves and our clients. After the markets, we visited the great Parisian department stores—Galleries Lafayette, Le Bon Marché, and Printemps—to see the latest styles. Visiting department stores is a great way to find out what the majority of retailers are selling and what the majority of consumers are buying. And it's always interesting to see the displays. Exhausted, we headed back to the hotel for a light dinner and an early night.

The next morning, our first stop was to see our old friend Hélène, who does what we do but on a much smaller and more intimate scale. She is a one-woman business and deals exclusively in the top brands. She has a tiny little shop near Les Halles, the famous Paris meat market, where she quietly and discreetly buys and sells vintage and contemporary luxury handbags, jewelry, scarves, and a few clothing items, but mostly bags and accessories. She's come to be one of our best suppliers, and we always visit her when we are in Paris.

We had told her we were coming, and she had promised to set aside wonderful things for us. We knew that even if Georgette and her friends didn't turn out to have the goods, we could count on Hélène, who always had fabulous items we could buy and resell.

When we arrived, Hélène greeted us like the old friends we were. She put the *Fermé* sign on her door and led us through her tiny shop to her office in back, which was decorated in faded, *fin-de-siècle* splendor—worn Persian rugs, comfy armchairs, a Louis XV writing desk. She had laid out tea from Mariage Frères, one of the oldest and grandest tea purveyors in Paris, and a little platter of madeleines, those delicious little lighter-than-air cookies that melt in your mouth. We chatted and gossiped and caught up on news: what was hot, what was not, what was selling, who was selling, who was doing well, who was not. We can always count on Hélène for great items and great gossip. She filled us in on who was selling and why, on the comings and goings of her clients, on the doings and happenings of couture Paris.

And then we got down to business. True to her word, Hélène had fabulous handbags for us. She showed us a dozen, and we bought four—an Hermès Kelly Bag, a Chanel cross-body bag, a Chanel tote, and a Chloé clutch—all in perfect condition. We gently haggled over the price. We are old pros at this. Diana and I know exactly what we need to spend or be paid to make it worth our time, and we each know the number we will settle on; but as a matter of courtesy, we haggled any-way. We paid $4,000 for four handbags that we later resold for $7,000. Already the trip had been worth it.

After lunch, we headed to see Georgette's friend Camille in the swanky eighth *arrondissement* on the right bank of the Seine. We were enthralled the minute we stepped out of the cab. Camille's apartment took up an entire floor of a centuries-old building, with commanding views of the Seine and the most beautiful sights in Paris. Camille greeted us at the door warmly but warily, as if she wasn't sure what she was getting herself into. She was young, sophisticated, and charming. She explained that she had never sold items before but that Georgette had recom-mended us highly. We put her at ease like the pros we were.

Camille led us to a light-filled sitting room where she had laid out a number of items on an antique table. Everything was incred-ible, and we took almost all of what she was offering. We bought a Cartier watch, two Hermès scarves, and some very high-end, very fine jewelry, much of which had been made just for her. Jewelry, especially bespoke jewelry, can be tricky. Something that has been crafted specially for someone is often too unusual or too personal to be appealing to buyers. But Camille's pieces were exquisite, and we knew we could resell them easily. We were thrilled to buy them and thrilled with our great fortune.

And then came the handbags. Camille excused herself, left the room, and returned with several extraordinary items: a little camellia-embossed black lambskin Chanel wallet, which was and is a very hot item, always a top seller. Those fly out the door, and we bought it on the spot. We also bought a very unusual, very rare, vintage Chanel clutch, which we knew we could sell. It might take a while—not everyone is in the market for a vintage Chanel clutch—but we had a few clients in mind, collectors who we knew would love this particular item. Camille also offered us one of her three Hermès Birkin bags.

The Hermès Birkin bag is the most famous and coveted handbag in the world. It is THE statement handbag for fashionable and rich women around the world. It was created in 1984 and named after British actress Jane Birkin—the original "It Girl"—who inspired the roomy tote. The bags have reached iconic status around the world. Each is made to order, with a starting price tag of about $11,000. And because of their iconic status, they are always a great sell. We seek them out because they are so popular. Even at a starting resale price of $5,000 or so, we cannot keep them in stock.

The one Camille was willing to part with was the first one she had ever owned. It was eight years old (a gift from her husband on her thirtieth birthday), a classic orange 35-cm (the second-largest size available), in absolute mint condition. Original retail price? Almost $40,000. Camille wanted $35,000 for it.

We loved the bag and knew we could find a buyer for it, but only if we could get it for $8,000-$10,000. But Camille held firm on her price. I don't think she was really ready to part with it, and, quite frankly, I couldn't blame her. (We never, ever try to talk anyone into selling their items.) So, no sale on the Birkin, but we were thrilled with everything else we got.

We paid her, packed up our items, and headed back to the George V, where we freshened up and then set out to visit Anna, another friend of Georgette. Anna lived in the seventh *arrondissement* (where Karl Lagerfeld lives!) in a gorgeous, enormous house. (That's one of the tremendous benefits to our line of work — getting to see some of the world's most spectacular homes.)

Anna welcomed us and led us to her bedroom, where she had a few items laid out for us. Anna had several absolutely beautiful Loro Piana cashmere sweaters and five Louis Vuitton items — three small handbags and two wallets. The Loro Piana was wonderful, the cashmere just incredible. We knew we wouldn't get a lot for them — Loro Piana isn't a well-known name here in the States — but they were too beautiful to leave behind. The Louis Vuitton items, on the other hand, we knew we could do very well on, and that they would fly out of our store. We made an offer for all of it, and she accepted without negotiation.

We spent about $4,500 on items that ultimately netted about $5,500, so good but not great. We had one more of Georgette's friends to see in Paris, and she lived right around the corner from Anna.

Babette met us at the door of her apartment, and she was all business. She took us to her closet, where she had items laid out. She lifted each item in turn, described it, and told us what she had paid for it and what she wanted for it. She was really into her things, and I got the sense that this wasn't going to work out too well. Even if I gave her half of what she wanted, I couldn't make any money. It was a tough situation.

Most of Babette's things were straight from the runway or the atelier. They were items that models had worn in a runway show or couture items crafted for her. But not everyone is interested in couture or runway, and not everyone is as big around as a twig, so size is an issue, too. She had a beautiful leather jacket straight from Rick Owens's runway (retail: $2,000), a stunning Valentino overcoat (retail: $7,000), a Valentino dress (retail: $4,000), an Yves Saint Laurent suit (retail: $3,500), a Gucci dress (retail: $2,000), and more.

She wanted 80 percent or more of what she had paid, and that was just not going to happen. She started to get annoyed with us, as if we didn't understand what the items were worth, how special they were. I was, as always, incredibly gracious and polite.

I said, "Thank you so much, and please understand this is not personal. It's business. You paid a lot of money for your beautiful things, and you're entitled to ask whatever you like. But if I can't make any money, then I can't buy it. It's that simple."

We said goodbye to Babette and returned to the hotel for some much needed rest. Buying gorgeous items can be exhausting!

The next morning, we got up early to get ready for our meeting with Georgette. After croissants and café au lait in our sunny suite, we were off. She and her husband lived in a wonderful neighborhood in the fourth *arrondissement* called the Marais. The Marais is at once aristocratic yet funky and cool.

We rang the bell, and a maid in a sleek, chic black outfit opened the door. "Bonjour," she said, "Madame is expecting you. Follow me please." (I wish I would have taken a picture of the maid's outfit. No fussy starched dress/apron combo here; her outfit looked like it had been designed by Armani.) We entered the house, and what I saw literally took my breath away.

At this point in my life, I am a hard woman to impress. I've seen everything, from squalor to splendor. I've been in some of the most beautiful homes in the world, but this house was *magnificent*. The outside was subtle and elegant, with that placid, Parisian old-world charm. You pass by exteriors like this a dozen times a day in good French neighborhoods. But the inside was absolutely stunning.

The floors were burnished parquet. The ceilings looked to be about twenty-five feet high, with French doors (naturally) letting in gobs of sunlight and allowing spectacular views of the neighborhood. The white walls were covered with the most extraordinary collection of modern art I had ever seen outside a museum. I recognized Chagall, Rothko, Jasper Johns, and others. The entire effect was breathtaking.

The maid led us to a first-floor sitting room where Georgette was waiting. She greeted us politely but curtly. Despite the fact that we had opened our store for her an hour early for her to shop privately, she was not very friendly. She wanted to get down to business, and do it quickly.

She ushered us out of the sitting room, through the house, and up a staircase. Diana and I craned our necks as we went, our eyes popping out of our heads each time we peered down a hallway or into a room and saw some fabulous work of art or gorgeous piece of furniture. There was some construction going on in the house, so many things were covered in plastic sheeting and a few rooms were closed off, but we still ogled everything as we went along.

Georgette led us to an enormous dressing room on the second floor, where dozens of items were set out for us to look at. Boxes of Manolo Blahnik and Christian Louboutin pumps, Valentino dresses and jackets, Chanel suits, blouses by Céline and Chloé. It was an amazing treasure trove, and I began wondering how I was going to get all those shoeboxes on the flight home.

Just then a dashing, elegantly dressed, slightly older man came in. "Ah, darling!" Georgette said. "Ladies, this my husband, François."

He was movie-star handsome, elegant, and sophisticated, like a French Jeremy Irons. And when he walked into the room, Georgette's entire demeanor changed. A moment before she had been curt, all business, even a little icy. Now, in front of François, she was coy and playful and affectionate, stroking his arm and back. She was coquettish and sweet, all smiles, and glowing with affection.

"You are the Americans I have heard so much about," François said. "I am so glad you could come. My wife is ready to part with some of her lovely things, and I hear you are the best in the business. My wife has so many beautiful things, we are building more closets for her."

The dressing room we were in was about 500 square feet; it was one of the biggest dressing rooms I'd ever been in. And they were building more?

François then led us through a history of Georgette's things, item by item. Clearly, he cherished these items and cherished the memories of where he had purchased them for his lovely (and much younger) wife and where she had worn them. He held up a red silk Valentino dress and explained, "I bought this dress for her in Los Angeles, and when she wore it, every head in the room turned." He held up a pair of sky-high Louboutins and said, "We bought these in New York, remember darling? My God, when she wore these shoes, she looked like a goddess."

It became very clear, very quickly that he adored his wife and loved to dress and accessorize her with the very best that money could buy. And Georgette played right along. She was far too sophisticated to giggle, but she was sweet and doting and hung on his every word.

François continued to regale us with stories of these gorgeous things. He was just darling with her, and she was darling with him. Every once in a while, they would whisper coy little things to each other in French and nuzzle each other. They were very affectionate, almost to the point where it got a little uncomfortable and embarrassing to be in the same room with them. Then, he was done.

"Ahh!" he exclaimed, looking at his elegant Patek Philippe watch. "Ladies, as much as I would love to stay here all day with you, someone's got to work!" And with that we all shook hands, he kissed his wife, nuzzled her neck, and left.

As soon as he was gone, Georgette's demeanor immediately became cool. Once again, she was all business. It was remarkable. She was not the same person as when he was in the room. It was like a freeze came over everything. She said, "So here are these things, and I have other things for you to see as well. Follow me."

We hustled down another long hallway, to the back of the house and up another flight of stairs. She opened a door and we entered another, slightly smaller but still very large dressing room. And the clothes in this room were *completely*, wildly different. I mean, and pardon my French, everything was slutty! This was very racy, sexy stuff. And I don't mean Versace or Gucci racy. I mean Frederick's of Hollywood racy. Not at all the cool, classic elegance of the other closet. No, this stuff was hard-core sexy, with a little light bondage thrown in. I was thinking this closet must belong to their daughter, but then I remembered that they had no children.

Georgette said she'd like to get rid of most of the items, and Diana and I silently flipped through the racks and shelves. We didn't say a word, but our minds were racing, and we were trying not to look at each other. Then, Georgette said, "I wear these things when I visit my friend in Nice."

I said, "Oh, I see. Because these things are so different from your other closet."

Georgette replied, "Yes, she prefers that I dress a certain way. We have been together since college."

She? Oh, OK, so longtime lesbian lover. Got it. Now I'm thinking this might be the most interesting woman in the world. Married to a stunningly handsome, fabulously wealthy older man with a decades-long lesbian love affair on the side.

"See if there's anything in here you can use," Georgette said. "I'm done with all of this." And she walked out of the room. My mind started racing: Is her love affair over? Did it end badly? Are they still together but just past this sexy phase? What is the story here?

Diana and I looked at each other, stunned. We started furiously whispering to each other as we opened drawer after drawer of lace stockings, garter belts, camisoles, silk scarves, fluffy handcuffs, and more. It was crazy.

The maid came in and said, "Madame said to take what you want from this room and the first room and prepare your offer. Please let me know when you're ready."

There was very little we could use from the sexy room, but there was a tremendous amount of stuff in that first room that we wanted. We choose twenty pairs of shoes (mostly Manolos and Louboutins), several Valentinos, the Céline and Chloé blouses, the Chanel suits, Chanel jewelry, a dozen handbags, and a few dozen other items. We prepared our first offer.

Now, usually our thinking on offers is we're going to start here but we can go up here, if need be. Above all, the most important thing, always, is to make every client happy. Our objective is to help them get rid of the things they no longer want and to make them happy in the process. I never, ever, want to leave anybody uncomfortable or sad about selling their items, or feeling as though we've taken advantage of them. We always want to buy the come back, so we strive to be both generous and fair.

I told the maid we were ready, and she went to get Georgette. When she returned, I said, "Thank you so much for having us in your home. We've looked at your things, and these are the items that we're able to use. We can offer you this much." I can't remember what the exact figure was, but it was about $10,000. Without hesitation, she said, "Fine. Just get it out as quickly as possible and go. I have things to do." And that was it. We wrote her a check on the spot, and she disappeared.

Diana and I spent the next thirty minutes packing the items as quickly as we could. We are very methodical and efficient at this, but we were hurrying since it was clear that Georgette wanted us out of her house as soon as possible. The maid had called us a cab, and we ran back and forth, up and down the stairs, loading bags and boxes into the waiting taxi.

At one point, flustered and rushing with my arms full of shoeboxes, I took a wrong turn down a hallway, rounded a corner, and almost ran right into Georgette. She was pressed up against the wall with her leg wrapped around a young construction worker. They were in a *very* intimate, very passionate embrace. I said, "Oh!" and dropped the boxes I was carrying.

Georgette glared at me. "Aren't you finished yet?" she said. I scrambled away as fast as I could.

When we had loaded the last bag into the cab, I thought about finding Georgette to thank her. But better sense prevailed and we left quickly and quietly. We sent her flowers and a thank-you note instead.

All in all, our Paris buys netted us plenty to cover the trip and make a very nice profit. *Magnifique*!

Will Travel for Louis: Tips for a Closet Buy

We look at 1,000 pieces a day at the Vault Luxury Resale in Saint Louis, so we really don't need to travel for items. That said, we are more than happy to come to your house to do a closet buy if you've got the goods, by which we mean so many fabulous bags, shoes, jewelry, and clothes that you can't possibly make it in. But before you call, here's some advice:

- **Know what we want.**
  We want labels from the better department stores and boutiques purchased in the last two years. We want handbags, shoes, jewelry, and clothing from Chanel, Louis Vuitton, Gucci, YSL, Hermès, Tory Burch, Kate Spade, Marc Jacobs, David Yurman, Stella McCartney, Lululemon, Athletica, J Crew, Eileen Fisher, Vince, Theory, and the like.

- **Know what you're selling.**
  We will prequalify over the phone, so be sure you have an accurate list of the items—label, item type, etc. For the very high-end purchases, we will need to authenticate every item, so if you have receipts, authenticity cards, and the original packaging, that is always very helpful.

- **Be organized and ready.**
  While we certainly don't mind perusing your entire closet, the buy will go much more smoothly and quickly if you pull out ahead of time the items you want us to look at. Be ready for us!

Chapter Seven
Twerkin' for a Birkin and Favors in Florence

When I say we deal with women from all walks of life, I really mean it. Two closet buys from 2011 reveal just how diverse our clientele is.

In Saint Louis, we had a client, Miranda, from whom we bought many gorgeous handbags. A beautiful young woman, she came into the store four or five times over the course of about two years. She was lovely, elegant, sophisticated, and far too young to have bags like the ones she was selling us. Her items were the most up-to-date and fabulous handbags out there—the very latest from Louis Vuitton, Fendi, Marc Jacobs, and, the most coveted of all, an Hermès Birkin bag. She lived in Saint Louis but she traveled constantly. Naturally, we never asked what she did or how she came to own these beautiful bags. We assumed she was a very (very!) successful pharmaceutical rep or something like that.

That winter, Diana and I went to Las Vegas for a big wholesale show. In the airport, we ran smack into Miranda. "What are you doing here?" we asked her. Miranda told us she had an apartment in Vegas and lived there part time. She was thrilled to run into us, she said, because she had a few more handbags to sell; would we mind popping up to her apartment while we were in town? She also said she had several colleagues who would love to meet us and sell their handbags, too. Diana and I said sure, and we arranged to meet her and her friends the next day.

When we got to Miranda's apartment, she and her friends were waiting for us. They were drinking champagne and having a good time. They talked about their clients, some of whom they shared. They gossiped about who saw who in LA or New York, who saw who in the Bahamas or Jamaica: "I saw Henry in Nassau last month, and he was with Betsy." "Really? I saw him in Palm Springs, and he was with Amber!" We never discussed the specifics of their line of work, but it became pretty clear that these ladies were not sales reps for Merck.

A few minutes later, there was a knock at the door, and a striking young woman in a form-fitting Azzedine Alaia dress and heels burst in. She had eight fabulous handbags draped on her arms. One of the girls squealed with delight and said, "Ooooh, Tara girl, you been fucking!" Not a sales rep.

The girls had amazing bags. Few things radiate wealth, status, and taste more than a handbag. One look at a woman's bag speaks volumes about her, and often about the men they are with. These were smart women; they knew that their handbags were status symbols, and they owned the biggest Louis Vuitton bags, the Guccis with the biggest Gs, the Pradas with the biggest tags, and, of course, Birkins. They wanted to be seen with the best bags. And their clients did, too, because the bag their woman carried spoke volumes about them as well.

Another reason these girls carried such fabulous bags is that they were savvy about making as much money as possible:

Very often, their clients would give them credit cards to go shopping, and they would go right to Chanel, Hermes, Saint Laurent, Gucci, or Louis Vuitton and buy the most expensive bag in the store. They would carry the bag for a while and then flip it for oodles of money. They didn't have any allegiance to the bag or the brand. These were commodities to them, and they knew that these high-caliber bags kept their value. Reselling the bags was a smart way for them to make even more money from their clients and further monetize the relationships. These were clever girls.

They had an uncanny instinct for resale, which made our job very easy. I gladly bought their bags. We left there with thousands of dollars in handbags and some very happy new customers. What happens in Vegas doesn't always stay in Vegas. Sometimes it makes its way to the Vault.

Florence, Italy, is about as far from Las Vegas as you can get in terms of style and substance, and our 2011 closet buy there was as far from our Vegas experience as you can imagine. Shortly after Diana and I returned from Vegas, I got a call from a very good client in Chicago, a wealthy, aristocratic Italian woman from whom we had bought many beautiful things. She had a sister in Florence who was ready to part with some items of high value, and she was wondering if we'd be interested. We did our due diligence; contacted the sister, who sent photos and information to us; and we decided it was worth our time and expense to fly to Florence.

When we travel overseas for a buy, we try to arrive at least two days prior to our appointment. That way, we can settle in, recover from jet lag, and scope out where we'll be going. This meeting was to take place at our client's home outside Florence.

We rented a car and drove out of the city, across the Arno, and into the countryside. About twenty minutes later, we found the client's house. It was exactly what you think a traditional Italian villa should look like. The house was set back from the road, and we turned onto a drive lined with majestic cypress trees. We pulled up, rang the bell, and a servant ushered us in.

We stepped into the house and realized that the front view gave only a hint of what the house was really like. The entire back of the house was constructed of glass, with sweeping, unobstructed views of terraced vineyards and lawns, and, in the distance, the Arno River and Florence.

The house was about 400 years old, but the interior and the back of the house had been renovated extensively by someone with a very modern eye. On the first level was the kitchen, family living room, formal living room, and an expansive terrace with sweeping views. On the upper levels were bedrooms, and on the lower level were the servants' quarters. The housekeeper, cook, and gardener lived on site.

Diana and I stood with our mouths open, taking it all in — the view, the furniture, the art. The interior was white on white, with traditional Italian Renaissance art mixed with Cubist treasures, big white rugs with antique furniture. We were speechless, and by this time we had seen some of the most beautiful homes in the world.

A few moments later, our new client appeared. She was beautiful, late-fifties, dressed stylishly but not ostentatiously. She wore a simple but luxurious Prada dress and pumps, with the perfect amount of jewelry. She was the epitome of elegance, of Italian aristocracy.

In my opinion, the Italians have a more subtle elegance than the French. French women might throw in an accessory or something that gives an outfit a little bit of an edge, a tiny kick. Italian elegance is a little more understated, conservative, and old-world.

Here's an example: Once when we were in Italy in a little café, an old woman was cleaning the steps of the cathedral next door. She was wearing pumps, stockings, a well-cut wool skirt, and a beautiful, if old, blazer. She looked as elegant as if she were going to lunch. That's old-world elegance. That's Italy for you.

Our new client looked like Sophia Loren, so we dubbed her Sophia. Her English was, of course, perfect. She invited us in to the living room, where we sat to take in the view. A few moments later, the servant appeared with tea. I didn't know where to look —at my beautiful new client or the spectacular view. At the art on the walls or the centuries-old furniture?

Sophia was as gracious as could be. She wanted to know all about us, our trip, where we were staying, our business, our families, other clients. We asked her all about her family and her house, and we talked and talked. No one mentioned why we were there. We've learned that you cannot rush these things, and you must take your cues from your client. And Sophia was in no hurry.

The more we talked, the more we fell in love with her, with her house, and with Italy. At one point, her two sons came in to meet us. They were young and handsome, late twenties, dressed beautifully, with that sense of *sprezzatura* — nonchalant, almost careless elegance—that only Italians can pull off. We were dazzled by them, and it was clear that they were dazzled by their mother. They met us and embraced her lovingly. One said to me, "Don't you think my mother is beautiful?" It was very sweet and very genuine. They were gorgeous, their mother was gorgeous, the house was gorgeous. We were giddy!

The boys said that it was time for lunch, so the five of us walked through the kitchen and out to a terrace, where we were served lunch overlooking the vineyard. Diana and I were completely enchanted. It was truly one of the best days of my life.

Sophia was as fascinated with me as I was with her. She wanted to know how my business worked and what it was like to be a business woman in America. We talked about our children, current events, fashion, politics, everything under the sun. We were both well-traveled women, and we talked about where we'd been and what we'd seen and what should be done in the world. Diana and her sons took it all in, and we were all smitten with each other.

We had wine with lunch, which lasted two hours. Then we went back inside and had coffee. After that we got a tour of the house and the grounds, which were magnificent, and then took a nice, long stroll. We repaired back to the living room where we had cocktails. After cocktails, it was dinner time. We went back out to the terrace, and, as we were walking, Sophia took my arm and whispered in my ear, "After dinner, I have a few things I would like you to look at."

I looked at her quizzically for a moment. I had no idea what she was talking about. Then I remembered: the closet buy. Of course! I was having such a wonderful time with this woman and her family that I had completely forgotten why we were there.

Over dinner, we talked more about Italy and about her family and its history. The house had been in her family for centuries. Her family had a long involvement with the arts and with law and politics. They knew the Ferragamos and all the best families in Italy. We talked and talked and talked. Unlike the women we had dealt with in Paris, Sophia would not be rushed. This wasn't business for her; it was personal.

But finally, dinner was over, the *digestifs* had been poured, and we went back inside the house. Sophia led Diana and me up the stairs, down a winding hallway, and into her master bedroom, where one walk-in closet was inside another. The inner sanctum of the inner sanctum. It was stunning, more like a chic museum than a closet. Ferragamo scarves were displayed on beautiful racks and framed on the wall. She touched each one and told us its history: her first scarf, a gift from her mother; the first scarf she ever bought herself; the first one her husband bought her; one that had belonged to her grandmother. Sophia was reverential about them.

Then we talked about a few things in her closet. She said, "I'm not a flashy dresser." That was obvious. She bought things for the quality and then kept them forever. She didn't have a lot of clothes but she had a lot of shoes, absolutely beautiful shoes. And like the Ferragamo scarves, they were displayed like the works of art they were. Sophia respected craftsmanship, and her closet was a testament to that. The shelves had been specially constructed to house her heels, and they were displayed with museum-like precision and care. She pulled out a half dozen heels she was interested in parting with, and then she pulled clothes from her racks. A Chanel jacket, a few Prada skirts, two Miu Miu dresses, an Hermès blouse, Loro Piana sweaters, a few Fendi items, some handbags, and more. She explained each piece to us.

Her things were beautiful, but she pulled out many items that we couldn't use because they were too old, too obscure, or too out of style. But Diana and I knew that rather than insult her, we would take everything. The Chanel jacket was very sellable. The Ferragamo loafers, not so much; they were too worn. But there were a few Ferragamo bags that were fabulous. The Prada skirts were probably a little too old. The Loro Piano cashmere, maybe.

When we finished in Sophia's closet, she said, "I have some other things I want to show you that have been in my family forever, but they aren't anything that we could ever enjoy. We didn't come by them the way you would like to come by things."

We didn't quite follow her, but she explained: "During World War II, some of my family were very involved in the politics of the war. One of those people was my grandmother." She showed us a picture of her grandmother from the early 1940s. She was stunning, a real Italian beauty.

"My grandmother was very social, very well connected, and very involved in the politics of the time. She had friends in the resistance movement and friends who were aligned with Mussolini. She was young and smart and beautiful, and she was always invited to the right parties with the right people in the right places. Since she was friendly with both sides, she was an appealing person to many in power. She was wooed by both sides."

"She gave the resistance information, and she gave the fascists information, just enough so both sides would trust her. It worked well for her. In fact, she was so successful that her benefactors showered her with gifts. And these are the items that we no longer want to keep."

Sophia showed us these gifts: a gorgeous hand-painted silk shawl, a small leather case, a silver box, a silver cigarette case with jeweled inlay, a crocodile handbag, and magnificent jewelry, some of which was original Tiffany and some original Coco Chanel from the 1930s.

"Of course, we could never enjoy these things," Sophia said. "We certainly could never use them or wear them, but they are much too nice to just get rid of. We've kept these things all these years because what else could we do with them? My grandmother hid them away. They passed to my mother, who hid them away, and then they came to me. I've been hiding them for years, and I would like for you to take them to America, away from here. Buy them from us, and we will donate the money to charity, so we can do some good."

Diana and I were a little stunned by this. What exactly were we buying? But the pieces were extraordinary. We made an offer and she accepted. We saw the immediate relief on her face. There was shame there, and utter relief when we took them off her hands. She had to cleanse her family's conscience.

We were finished. By now it was 10 p.m. It had a been a long but wonderful day, with a twist ending we never saw coming. Sophia insisted on having her staff pack everything for us and ship it to Saint Louis. When the pieces arrived a week or so later, each was individually wrapped with a handwritten card explaining the piece and its provenance: Chanel jacket, 2001, purchased in Milan. Ferragamo bag, custom order, 2004. Fendi baguette, 2003, purchased in Florence.

We must have broken the spell of the bad karma around those items, because they sold almost immediately. We didn't make much money on that trip, but we made Sophia very happy—and, hopefully, we were able to help clear the air of that bad juju.

A week after we got back Diana, turned to me and said, "I don't know what was more interesting, the escorts in Vegas or the aristocrats in Florence, but this sure is a fascinating business!" I couldn't agree more.

Sue says

"Good better best. Never let it rest until the good is the better and the better is the best."

"If it's not becoming on you, it should be coming to me."

"Nothing sells like a good reputation."

"Change is hard and uncomfortable. It's much easier to do nothing and accept the status quo. You sit in your shit because it's warm."

"It's only worth what we can sell it for. And it's not worth anything gathering dust in your closet."

"Kindness and generosity are always in fashion."

Woman looking at herself in mirror while trying on a spectacular Lilly Pulitzer dress: "I don't really need this."

Sue: "Darling, if you only bought what you needed, you'd be a man."

Chapter Eight
Resale Royalty

I have always thought that my business is interesting. It combines retail with treasure hunting, fashion with passion, and business with pleasure. Every day is like Christmas; we get to open presents! We never know what will walk in that door or what we will find in a closet. It's fun and fabulous.

I always thought that what we did would make a great reality TV show. Our business has everything a producer could want: behind-the-scenes action, treasure hunting, bargaining, fashion makeovers, and the potential for family, customer, and employee drama and hurt feelings. Plus, it's different every day. Every seller is a story, every buy is a risk, and every day is a new day in the world of luxury resale.

And our clients are wonderful women with great personalities, like the women who shop just to spend money, with no intention of ever wearing their items. Then they bring their items to us, price tags still on, and don't bat an eyelash when we pay them a fraction of the retail price. And there are the young women who save up and come in for their first Louis Vuitton bag. Precious.

Every day, we have phenomenally interesting people we're dealing with and fantastically wonderful items we are buying and selling. We're doing closets all over the world, taking in over 500 items a day, and, in my mind, we are so much more interesting than 95 percent of what's out there on reality TV.

So in 2011, I pitched the idea of a show to my son-in-law, Jon Maurice, who's a partner in a Saint Louis-based production company, No Coast Originals. Jon liked the idea, and we pitched it to another local production company, Coolfire Originals. My pitch was honest and passionate. I knew my business was a great idea for a show, and I let that speak for itself. I made it clear that I didn't need more money or more business, and I certainly was not courting fame. I wanted to do this because I thought it would make for great television, and I wanted to represent the resale industry in a good light. As a proud, long-standing member and former vice president of the National Association of Resale Professionals, I wanted to show the resale industry with great integrity. I had seen other shows where buyers tried to talk people out of their items. That's not how responsible resellers operate.

I also wanted to show women doing the right thing — working together, being profitable, being fair and kind, being supportive and generous. And it's so much fun! Every day we go home saying, "OMG, can you believe that happened? That was crazy! And that closet, can you believe we did that closet?" It was lady porn, really. That's what I pitched to a room full of men, and they got it.

The two companies teamed up, and we filmed a terrific sizzle reel. A sizzle reel is a short video, usually ten to twelve minutes long — sort of like a pilot. Production companies take sizzle reels to networks to get financing so they can produce their series. Hundreds of shows are pitched every year, but very few get the green light. And just because a show gets the green light for production doesn't mean it will air. But I knew ours would be chosen.

Jon and the guys from Coolfire took the sizzle reel to New York and Los Angeles, where they shopped it around. The Style Network said they were really interested in it, which I was thrilled about. That's who I wanted from the get-go, because it went with our brand. The Style Network (now defunct, sadly) was all about fashion, design, styling, and the like. It was a perfect fit for us.

As they were trying to sell the show, Jon recommended we get an agent, so we talked with folks at William Morris Endeavor (WME). We found an agent, who flew to Saint Louis to meet with us and sign papers. He told us that one of WME's clients was celebrity stylist Rachel Zoe, who had her own very popular reality TV show, *The Rachel Zoe Project* on Bravo, plus a great business as a designer, writer, and stylist. He said Rachel had her own production company, and he would pitch her the idea of coming on board as executive producer of our show.

"Rachel Zoe is going to love you," he said. "She is all about fashion and luxury for every woman, and she's all about family. She is going to love that about you, and I can see her really getting behind this project." He promised to pitch it to her and get back to us. But we didn't get our hopes up.

Weeks went by. We heard that they showed the sizzle reel to Rachel and Roger Berman, her husband and business partner, and that they loved it. But nothing concrete was happening. So we did what we do best: we worked. Diana had a shopping tour booked to New York City, and Laura and I went along. While we were in the airport, Laura read that Rachel, who lived in California, was going to be in New York that week hosting an event for Fashion Week.

"Oh, my God," Laura said. "Rachel Zoe is going to be in NYC the same time we are!"

I said, "That's fabulous! We are going to meet her."

Laura scoffed, "Sure, Mom. Nine million people in New York City, and we are just going to bump into her. Right."

"This is a perfect time for us to meet Rachel," I said. "and we are going to meet her." I know this in my mind. I can see it.

We arrived in New York and did our thing: shopping with Diana's tour group in the wholesale district and resale shops, dining out, walking everywhere. On the last night, we went to the Meatpacking District to have dinner with our group. It happened to be Fashion Week, so everywhere we went there were models and editors and designers and photographers. It was a mad house. As we were walking into the restaurant with our group, we noticed a huge crowd across the street, with cameras everywhere and a line of people waiting to get in. I asked the maître d' what was happening, and he said Rachel Zoe and her team were hosting a party at Intermix over there.

I looked at Laura and Diana, and I said, "See, I told you we were going to meet Rachel."

"Mom, there are a thousand people over there waiting on the sidewalk trying to get in," Diana said. "There are doormen with clipboards! You're nuts."

"Look at this coincidence that we're right across the street!" I said. "Believe me, it's going to work."

I sent Diana into the restaurant with her tour group and grabbed Laura's hand. "You're coming with me," I said and headed across the street.

Laura fought me the whole way. "This is crazy! We're not going to get in! Look at all those people!"

There was a huge crowd waiting to get in. It was mostly press, but there were lots of fashionistas, too. People in line were shouting at the doormen: "I'm on the list!" "Rachel is expecting me!" "I'm with *Women's Wear Daily*!" "I'm a blogger for *Elle*!" It was madness.

I worked my way to the front of the crowd, Laura in tow, and I stood calmly, quietly, and respectfully in front of the giant man with the clipboard. I didn't say a word. I just smiled pleasantly at him. He looked at me for a minute, then said, "You can go in." He lifted the rope, and in we went. Laura was stunned.

Inside it was bananas (to use one of Rachel's favorite expressions). Wall-to-wall people. Laura shouted, "Now what?"

"Just stick with me," I shouted back.

I snaked my way through the crowd, zigging and zagging until I spotted Rachel and Roger in a corner, where they were taking questions from the press. Lights were blazing on them as cameras flashed. People were being held back by a security team. I tightened my grip on Laura's hand and eased myself through the crowd until we were closer to the front. Roger was saying something into a camera when he spotted me.

"Oh, my God, that's Sue McCarthy!" he said, and he seemed genuinely pleased as punch. When she heard him, Rachel turned to look. "Oh, my gosh!" she said. "Let them in! Let them in!" The security team ushered us in.

"We saw the sizzle reel, and we loved it!" Rachel said. "We love you, we love your family, we love your business."

Roger swept his arm across the room and said, "Do you see this crowd? People are going to love you and your daughters. That show is going to be a hit, and there will be a crowd like this trying to interview you guys."

Laura and I were thrilled, and a little stunned at the attention! Rachel and Roger invited us to their hotel for dinner the next night, and Rachel agreed to come on board as executive producer. Once she signed on as EP, the Style Network pulled the trigger and ordered ten episodes. We had ourselves a TV show.

Things moved pretty quickly after that. Within a few months, there were production people everywhere. We loved the crew. They were phenomenal and phenomenally experienced. We started shooting in the fall and shot all ten episodes over the next eight months, with twelve- to sixteen-hour days the norm. It was exhausting, but fun and exciting, too.

The show centered around the store—the three of us, the staff, the sellers who walked in, special events, and a few big-time closet buys. A typical episode featured at least three walk-ins, where clients would come in with items to sell. There would be authentication and then negotiation. It's the same process every time, but it's different every time because no two items and no two customers are the same. We filmed behind the scenes in our office as we planned for special events. We filmed closet buys at the homes of some incredibly fabulous local women and clients in New York. One of our episodes was about theft in our stores. We hired a security expert to come in and help us. He brought in fake shoppers, who ended up stealing tons of merchandise right under our noses and right on camera. It was good television.

The girls and I had always done press, so we were used to being on camera. And it's amazing how quickly you get used to being followed around all day and night with a camera in your face and a microphone down your shirt. There were some really good characters on our staff who participated and really enjoyed it: JoJo, Jordan, and Molly, to name a few. And one of our staffers, Meghan King, went on to become a star on Bravo's *Real Housewives of Orange County*. After filming our show, Meghan met baseball great Jim Edmonds. They married and moved to LA, where they starred on the popular TV series.

Like the merchandise we sell, everything we did on camera was authentic. In the realm of reality TV, there's so much that is completely fake, believe me. But what we did was real. Those were real customers, real negotiations, and real closet buys.

When we did a closet buy on the show, we didn't meet the person or see the items in their closets until everything was in place and the cameras were ready to roll. In other words, we didn't arrive ahead of time and plan anything out or meet the client. Our crew went ahead and set everything up. When the cameras rolled and we said "Hi" to that person, that was truly the first time we met.

Each episode featured a fabulous closet buy, and two of the greatest closets we've ever done were featured on the show. (We never buy and tell, but because these closets and clients were featured on the show, we can use their names.) The first was a closet owned by the incomparable and unbelievably stylish Annie Brahler (now Annie Smith), one of the world's leading stylists and interior designers. We did not know Annie before the show, but she is a fixture in the design world here in Saint Louis and abroad. Annie owns Euro Trash, a company that offers exquisite, one-of-a-kind finds from Europe, as well as interior design, event design and production, personal styling, and professional styling for photo shoots and editorials. When she called to ask if we would do her closet, we were thrilled. And true to form, her closet did not disappoint (it's in episode one). It was the most amazing closet I had ever seen (until I saw Dr. Maude Kandula's closet in episode five!). The day we filmed that buy was the longest production day of the shoot. We were up almost twenty-four hours.

We were up at 6 a.m. or so and ready to start filming by 8 a.m. The closet buy was scheduled for the early evening, after work, and we had to drive to Annie's house, which was an hour away. The store closed at 5 p.m., and I figured we'd be at Annie's by 6 p.m., be done by 7:30 or 8 p.m., then go have dinner and be home by 10 p.m. But it was a cold, rainy night, there were production delays, and everyone was running late. We ended up sitting in our car for three hours while the crew finished setting up inside Annie's house. I think it was about 10 p.m. before we went in and started filming.

We were exhausted and starving, but we perked up the minute we stepped through her door. Her house was just gorgeous. White is Annie's signature color, and she employs it in the most beautiful way. There were different shades of white everywhere, with furniture and objets d'art placed just so. She had champagne for us, and we toasted to what we hoped would be a beautiful relationship. (Once the TV show aired, the champagne thing caught on, and now people offer us champagne wherever we go!)

Annie had set out wonderful food for us, but we didn't eat because we were on camera (the crew devoured everything anyway). Annie led us up the white staircase to her closet, and it was as if the angels sang. Annie is a professional stylist, and her closet was styled to perfection. It was merchandised like a showroom.

By now, it was about midnight, but we were wide awake as we went through Annie's things: Louis Vuitton handbags, Chanel bags, Burberry, Prada, Tom Ford, Vera Wang, Marc Jacobs. You name it, Annie had it. We were tired, we were hungry, and it was midnight on a stormy night, but we knew we had hit the jackpot. If you watch the episode, you can see how truly blown away we were by Annie's closet. It was incredible, and her items were extraordinary. She had every label we were seeking, and she was ready to part with a lot of it.

We ended up buying $15,000 worth of items — a huge buy for us. Every item was top quality, in perfect condition, and sellable the minute it hit the floor. We got home about 3 a.m., exhausted. But it was absolutely worth it.

One of my favorite segments of *Resale Royalty* was when we met and worked with Susan Sherman, Saint Louis's most fashionable woman and one of the most forward-thinking and dynamic women I have ever met. A force in fashion, art, society, and business, she is the CEO of Susan Sherman Inc., a PR firm, and co-founder and board chair of the Saint Louis Fashion Fund, which is single-handedly responsible for resurrecting the fashion industry here in Saint Louis. Susan is a huge supporter of the arts and is incredibly well-connected. Her circle of friends and acquaintances includes powerful people, movers and shakers, and fashionistas from New York to LA.

Susan had been a customer of ours when she first moved to Saint Louis from New York, so she was familiar with our business. She hadn't been in the store for a few years when she saw an article on us that got her thinking. As a PR consultant and patron of the arts, Susan hosted lots of events at her home, from fundraisers to trunk shows. She thought it would be fun to host a private show and sale to introduce us to her circle of female friends—super-stylish women, top executives, socialites, and art and fashion patrons. Susan is a connector. She loves to put people together, and we were thrilled with her idea.

We were excited, but we were also nervous. "We have got to get this right," I said to Diana. These were the most fabulous women in Saint Louis, and the pressure was on. (If you watch the episode, you can see how nervous we were. This was a really big deal for us!) We spent weeks getting ready for the event. Diana and Laura did a site visit to map everything out, and we asked Jordan and JoJo to "pull" for the event—to go through our inventory and pull out items that would appeal to this crowd. They pulled big-name labels—Armani, Gucci, Escada, Burberry, St. John—but Diana and Laura vetoed almost everything.

"Listen," Diana said. "This is a very chic crowd. These are the best-dressed women in Saint Louis, and they won't be wowed just by a label. The items have to be super stylish and fashion forward."

Diana then presented a rack of clothes that she and Laura had pulled to show the girls the difference. These items were from some of the same top labels—as well as edgier designers like Miu Miu, Pucci, Phillip Lim, Tom Ford, and others—but they were much more stylish, with sharper cuts, more interesting details, more unusual fabrics, and more stylish silhouettes. "Think current, extraordinary, edgy, cool," Diana admonished the girls. "Just say no-no to so-so."

Susan's gorgeous art-filled home in Saint Louis's most upscale neighborhood was the perfect venue. She invited about thirty women who came for cocktails and private shopping, and we brought our best merchandise, including jewelry, shoes, handbags, and clothes. (If you watch the episode you can see how much genuine fun everyone had.) And we sold over $8,000 worth of merchandise. We were all thrilled.

My favorite perq of being on *Resale Royalty* was when we got to go to New York Fashion Week, attend shows, and go backstage to meet designers. That was definitely Rachel Zoe's doing. She had the pull to make that happen. One of the shows we went to was the designer Lela Rose. Lela is a New York-based designer, born and raised in Texas. She's a good Texas girl who rides her bike with a big flower basket on it everywhere she goes in Manhattan. She is ladylike, sophisticated, and sweet, and her clothes are to die for. We were thrilled to meet her. She let us film at her show and surprised us by asking if we would do her closet. Naturally, we said of course!

The next day, we set out for her Tribeca townhouse in terrible weather. There was a huge snowstorm in New York, a virtual whiteout, and we were driving around with the film crew following us, trying to find Lela's townhouse. We finally got there and parked, and everyone was falling down in the snow and ice. We were in stupid six-inch heels, the camera crew was following us, and everyone was wiping out on the sidewalk. (You don't see that on camera!)

Lela's house was massive, maybe 5,000 square feet. Now the cameras were rolling. Lela graciously invited us in, and we sat in her beautiful living room where she had champagne (naturally!) ready for us.

She pointed to a long, empty room and said, "This is my dining room." We thought that was odd, a dining room with no furniture, but she pushed a button, and the table rose from the floor. She said she had designed it that way so the room could function for a dinner party or a runway. Crazy!

Then she took us to her closets—two of them, each on its own floor. Two whole rooms on two whole floors with hundreds of items. A lot of the items were her own samples from runway shows. Lela's aesthetic is very feminine and floral, and you can tell she's a Texan who dresses women like women. I love that about her. And the quality of her work is unparalleled.

In the first room, she pulled out about a dozen dresses for us to look at. Some were $2,000 dresses, and they were sample sizes, which means they were very, very small. We bought ten of those dresses, and the negotiating was interesting because we had to educate her a little bit on the reality of resale. She quickly understood the realities of our business, and we were able to come to good terms. She let us loose in her second closet and told us to choose whatever we wanted. We bought so much stuff that it took four girls several trips to carry everything out.

꙳ ꙳

Once filming wrapped, the network flew us to Los Angeles for "up fronts"—when networks introduce their new shows and new seasons of existing shows to the press. It's the industry's big dog-and-pony show, designed to show off its talent and TV lineup. The Style Network treated us like royalty (we were *Resale Royalty*, after all!). We were picked up at the airport by a black Escalade, put up in luxury suites, and given $400 a day (each!) per diem—not to mention hair, makeup, and wardrobe. Before we got there, we were coached by the producers in what to say and what not to say. We'd be in front of every press outlet you could think of, plus industry pros from every network and production company.

The day after we arrived, once we were primped, prepped, and camera-ready, the network executives led us out to the lawns, where the press outlets were gathered in little enclaves, each with its own tent. Here was *Variety*, there was the *Los Angeles Times*. Over there was *Entertainment Weekly* and *Entertainment Tonight*. We were led from tent to tent for interviews, each lasting about six minutes. The place was teeming with TV stars, all of whom were doing what we were—schlepping from tent to tent to pitch shows and impress the press. It was great fun.

During a break, I went back to the hotel in search of the bathroom. I was walking up the stairs when I saw gorgeous Heidi Klum coming down the stairs. She was an absolute vision, as stunning in person as she is on camera. As we passed in the middle of the staircase something came over me. I stopped her, took her hand, and said, "Oh, Heidi, I'm Sue McCarthy from Saint Louis. I'm here for my new show *Resale Royalty*, and I'm so pleased to meet you and am so grateful for the positive representation that you show to the young women of today."

As I was giving her all kinds of accolades, I reached up and brushed her hair out of her eyes. I'm a mother, and I can't help myself. I have to fix your hair if it's in your eyes. Meanwhile, Laura and Diana were at the bottom of the stairs watching me, shocked. Later, Laura said, "Mom! I can't believe you talked to Heidi Klum! And fixed her hair!" Someone snapped a picture of Heidi and me, and you can see how absolutely delighted I am to be with her.

One of the biggest episodes we filmed was when the girls surprised me with a twenty-fifth anniversary party at the Hilton in downtown Saint Louis. The day of the surprise party—and it was a real surprise—I had the flu and a fever of 102. I was in bed, sick as a dog, when one of the producers called and said, "Sue, you have to come to the Hilton downtown to film. It'll only take a few hours, but you have to be there."

I was green around the gills, sick as I've ever been, not even able to drive myself, but I pulled it together. A PA came and got me and drove me downtown. I didn't even ask why I needed to be there; I was told to be there and so I went.

One of the producers met me out front and was shocked to see how sick I was. She had to help me across the lobby I was so dizzy and weak, and before I could get into the elevator I threw up. We made it to the bathroom just in time. She was right there with me, fixing my hair and makeup and making me as presentable as possible. She felt so bad for me and said, "Sue, I am so sorry to put you through this, but it is really, really important. We will get you out of here as soon as possible."

She wouldn't tell me anything about what we were filming, only that I needed to go to the top floor. Once I was ready, they rolled camera and filmed me crossing the lobby and getting into the elevator. As soon as the doors closed, I slumped against the wall of the elevator. When I got to the top floor, I pulled myself together, took a deep breath, and walked out as soon as the doors opened. There was a camera right there to capture my every move. I exited the elevator, walked past the bar, parted a curtain, and heard, "Surprise!" There were my daughters, all of my employees past and present, plus my dearest friends and clients. I was totally shocked, and for the next hour my sickness was gone. I really enjoyed myself at that party, but the minute it was over, my flu came back, full force.

As I was making my way through the lobby on my way home, I knew I wasn't going to make it to the bathroom before I threw up. I had a cup in my hand, and I threw up right there into it, in the lobby of the Hilton. That's the glamorous life of a TV star for you. Luckily, the cameras didn't capture that little piece of cinema vérité.

The show aired in 2013, and it was an immediate hit. The ratings were great and people loved it. Our business doubled, and we were bursting at the seams. A year later, in 2014, we opened another store, the Vault Luxury Resale. In fact, the last episode of the series is us toasting to that new endeavor. We closed Clique, the teen boutique, and we added some of those teen brands into our general racks, so we had everything under one roof. So, in 2014, we had the original Women's Closet Exchange at one location and the Vault Luxury Resale with the Purple Cow children's boutique at the new one.

The Vault took off like a rocket. We designed it to be a little more curated, a little more high end, and very contemporary, with a gift boutique featuring new items as well as resale items.

We had come up with the idea for the Vault while filming. We always had more items than we could put on the floor at Women's Closet Exchange, and we kept those items in the "vault"—really just a part of the back office. Those items would eventually be put out, but that's how we got the idea of opening a second location and calling it the Vault. The season ended with us discussing opening the Vault, and within a few months it was a reality.

Before we could sign on to another season, there was a major shake-up and the Style Network dissolved. I'm not sure we would have signed up for another season anyway. It was a great experience and great for business, but it was invasive and intrusive. We had to eat, drink, and sleep our show, to the exclusion of everything else. We enjoyed it but we didn't need to do it again. I think we were all secretly relieved that there wouldn't be another season.

All in all, *Resale Royalty* was an incredible experience. I'm so grateful to my wonderful son-in-law for believing in me, for the producers and crew who made such an amazing, authentic show, and to all the fans out there who loved watching it. But no more TV for me.

Saint Louis: Fashion Capital

From the 1920s to the early 1950s or so, Saint Louis was home to the second-largest garment district in America, right behind New York. The epicenter was a fifteen-block stretch of Washington Avenue downtown, where thousands of people worked in more than 200 companies, designing, manufacturing, advertising, and selling the clothes that much of the country wore.

Back then, Saint Louis was famed for fashion, both in terms of the designs and innovations that were created here (two of the many advances to come out of Saint Louis were the shoulder pad and the designation of "junior" clothing, which became a huge share of the market) and the skilled hands that made the garments, not to mention the models who wore the clothes, the salesmen and advertising agencies that sold them, the photographers who photographed them, and the many other professions that supported—and were supported by— the fashion industry. Yes, Saint Louis meant Budweiser and the Cardinals, but fashion was an enormous part of the city's economy and an integral part of our identity.

When I was little, I remember walking down Washington Avenue with my sister and visiting the fashion houses. She was slim and trim and beautiful, and she modeled for a few of the companies. She took me along to her fittings and shopping trips, and it was an enchanting experience. Of course, by then—the late 1950s—many of the fashion houses and manufacturers had closed, but the street was still bustling. I remember the thrill of it, the hum of the sewing machines, the windows filled with beautiful dresses, the designers who doted on my sister, and the shoppers who ambled up and down the street. It was heady stuff, and I fell further in love with fashion.

By the early 1960s, however, the garment district in Saint Louis was virtually defunct. The designers had decamped for the coasts, and manufacturing had moved south or overseas to places where unions were nonexistent and labor was cheaper and faster. By the late 1960s, the garment district was gone, and Washington Avenue was a ghost town.

But now, things are changing. Not only has downtown Saint Louis seen an incredible revival in terms of housing and businesses, but a team of creative visionaries is working full time to bring fashion design and manufacturing back to Saint Louis.

In 2014, Susan Sherman (see page 100) and Tania Beasley-Jolly founded the Saint Louis Fashion Fund, a nonprofit dedicated to reviving the fashion industry here. In 2016, the Fashion Fund spearheaded a new initiative, the Saint Louis Fashion Incubator, and in January 2017 a class of six young designers was awarded two-year residencies at the Fashion Fund's stunning headquarters on Washington Avenue, in the heart of what was—and will be again—Saint Louis's garment district.

The designers, who were chosen by a panel of fashion veterans, each receive a stipend; are given offices, studio space, manufacturing space, and retail space; have access to state-of-the-art equipment; are provided with mentors, partnerships, and professional development opportunities; and are offered classes on marketing, branding, and other essential facets of the fashion business. The incubator is designed to give them space to design and create their garments and grow their businesses. We have high hopes that this is the start of something wonderful for Saint Louis fashion.

The six designers in the inaugural class are extraordinary talents, and I know their names will become as familiar to the country and the world as the Tory Burches, Vera Wangs, and Tom Fords of today. These young design talents are able to further hone their craft and grow their businesses thanks to the Fashion Fund:

- Agnes Hamerlik
- Emily Brady Koplar
- Allison Mitchell
- Audra Noyes
- Reuben Reuel
- Charles Smith II

We believe so strongly in the mission of the Saint Louis Fashion Fund that in 2016 we donated $10,000 to the organization, and my daughters, Diana and Laura, both served on the board of directors. We are proud supporters of this initiative to bring design and manufacturing back to our beloved home town of Saint Louis.

*Rachel Ray, me, Laura, and
Diana on the set, 2013*

With Oprah Winfrey, 2012

*With designer
Valentino, 2016*

With actress Jane Lynch, 2013

With model Heidi Klum, 2013

The Vault interior   Credit: Alex Johnmeyer; Super Keen Creations, LLC

Chapter Nine
The Actress & the Heiress

O nce the show aired, business really exploded. We were busy before, but now all four shops were jammed every day with buyers and sellers, and the phone rang off the hook with women calling to ask us if we would "do" their closets. Vetting and prequalifying intensified, and our criteria became even stricter.

In 2014, the year after the show aired, Laura and I were going to California on business. Before we left, I got a call from a man in Los Angeles who said his wife had several closets full of clothes that she wanted to get rid of. I prequalified the items, and the things he told me checked every box—labels like Gucci, Tom Ford, Chanel, Pucci, YSL, and Versace. He said that his wife had worked directly with many of the designers, who had custom-made clothes for her for premiers, red carpets, and other industry events. That piqued my interest. Even though, very often, custom-made items are a tough sell, I figured that if this woman—her husband never mentioned her name, or what she did—had custom items from those designers, the rest of her stuff would be great, too.

He also said that he and his wife were big fans of the show and that they particularly liked our professionalism and knowledge. Discretion was very important to him, and we assured him that, with the exception of the closet buys we did for our TV show, everything was confidential. As luck would have it, we were going to be in LA the following week, and I scheduled the closet buy.

When we got to California, we were busy every day in meetings and at events. On our last day, I told Laura that we were doing a closet buy that afternoon. She asked who it was, and I told her the man's name and that I didn't get the wife's name. "Mom, this could be a whack job and a complete waste of our time," Laura said. "Did you vet the items properly? Why didn't you speak to the woman herself, or let me do it?"

Laura was worried that some nut had seen the show and wanted to do who knows what to us. She was skeptical. But I had spoken to the husband and the items he described to me were right up our alley. I trusted him, and I told Laura to stop worrying and get in the car.

We drove to old Hollywood and pulled up to a gorgeous, gated, Spanish-style apartment complex. We were buzzed in, parked, and then took the elevator to the penthouse. We rang the bell, and the wife opened the door.

She was drop-dead beautiful. I was so struck by her beauty that I couldn't help myself, and I blurted out, "Oh, my God. Darling, you are so beautiful! You should be an actress!"

She was probably in her mid-forties and had obviously taken extraordinary care of herself. I didn't place her; I just knew she was incredibly beautiful. Her husband appeared and introduced himself. He was a very handsome guy, probably a little younger than his wife, and very gracious.

They invited us in and led us to a beautiful spread of champagne and fresh fruit. The two-level apartment was gorgeous, with white and pink marble everywhere. They told us how much they liked our show and asked how we liked being on TV. We jokingly complained about the long days of shooting, and the woman laughed and said, "Don't I know it!"

Laura said to her, "Yes—you would know about that!" Everyone laughed, and it became obvious to me that Laura knew who she was, but I still didn't.

They took us into a back room with two racks of clothing and two tables with purses, jewelry, scarves, and hats. The wife pointed out a few of her favorite items: "Armani made this for me, and I wore it to the Golden Globes. Valentino made this for me for the Emmy's. Oh, and Tom Ford designed this for me."

She smiled as she flipped through the racks, remembering where she had worn certain pieces and how she had felt wearing them. Laura went gaga over her hat collection and was particularly smitten with a black felt fedora with a leather feather. The woman picked it up, placed it on Laura's head, and said, "It's yours. My gift to you!" Laura was thrilled, and she still wears it every chance she gets.

The woman had seen the show and knew the drill, so she left us to look through everything and come back with a price. As soon as she left the room, Laura turned to me, grabbed my arm, and whispered, "OH, MY GOD! I can't believe we're doing her closet!"

I said, "Yes, she's very pretty and very stylish."

Laura narrowed her eyes and said, "Mom, you don't know who she is, do you?" I told her I didn't. She rolled her eyes and pulled out her iPhone. She went to Google images and pulled up a picture from 1992—one of the most iconic images in the world.

The light bulb went on, and I knew immediately who she was. This woman was one of the biggest stars on one of the world's most popular TV shows, which ran for about ten years in the 1990s. No wonder designers were making clothes for her. She was the all-American girl. She was on posters!

And everything was tailor-made for her when she was as big around as a toothpick. That's not to say that she was fat now. She looked fit, trim, healthy, and slender. But when she was on that TV show, she had to maintain a very, very sleek figure, and the clothes she wanted to get rid of were mostly from that era. I understood right away that she was a different person now, someone who didn't need to fit into a size double-zero and who wanted to unburden herself of her past. This was a catharsis for her, and I was happy to help.

She had come to the right place. She knew that it was best for her to sell her items somewhere besides LA, where someone might recognize a certain piece. She also knew she could trust us to keep it confidential. We never divulge whose items we have bought and sold. If people knew they were buying a certain celebrity's handbag, would we get a higher price? Would that bag have more interest to a buyer? Probably, but that isn't how we do business.

The actress had gorgeous clothes, mostly in very small sizes. And she had some great accessories, wonderful hats, jewelry, and belts. She had about eight clutches she wanted to sell and two Goyard totes. But the shoes were the real standouts.

She had great sandals, boots, and red-carpet ready heels by Stuart Weitzman, Badgley Mischka, and, of course, Jimmy Choo and Louboutin.

The shoes would sell themselves. The clothes were trickier. Generally, we like merchandise that we can put on the floor right away and sell. But with tiny, custom designer threads it's harder. In this case, though, the clothes were so exquisite and so special that we had a few clients — stylists and collectors — in mind who would jump at the chance to own these extraordinary items. These were rare pieces, and stylists often look for just such items for their clients who do not want to walk a red carpet or attend a premier wearing something that anyone could buy off the rack. We know our clients as well as our suppliers, so we know what to buy, and who to sell to. In this case, even though the clothes were very much specialty items, we knew we could move them. And the shoes, hats, and accessories were no-brainers.

The negotiation was easy. We wanted to make her happy, and, as always, we hoped she would tell her friends and think of us again. So, we went a little higher than normal. We wanted to be sure she knew how much we appreciated the opportunity. But it's not about the money; it's about what the money says. And in her case, it was really about moving on. She was done being in the spotlight. She was done killing herself to maintain an absurd weight. It was very symbolic.

She accepted our offer right away and said she was thrilled. We ended up buying fifty pieces from her. I stayed and talked to the couple while Laura packed everything and schlepped it to the car. (I am the schmoozer, not the schlepper.)

I wrote her a check, we said our good-byes, and Laura and I were on our way.

Within a month, we had sold all of her items, and no one who bought them knew they were wearing or carrying something that had belonged to one of the world's most famous TV actresses. That's the wonder of resale. You just never know.

Soon after the actress, we got call from a woman in Dallas. Chatty and charming, she regaled me with her shopping ethos and what was in her closet.

"Honey," she said. "I have a closet that is simply bursting at the seams! Nieman's is dead empty when I leave that store! My daughter said I have to get rid of everything and start over, so that's what I'm gonna do. We adore your show and would be so pleased if you could come on out. You can do my closet and my daughter's, and I promise you it'll be worth the trip."

I handed the phone to Laura for vetting, and her eyes got wider and wider as she took notes on what the woman said she had. Laura requested photos of the items, and within the hour, Dallas had emailed dozens of pics to us. Laura called her back to schedule the buy, and Dallas said her daughter would bring her things over to her house so we could do both buys there.

Even though it was only two closets, it sounded like a lot of merchandise, and we had wanted to make a trip to Texas to hit the wholesale markets and resale shops in Dallas and Houston, so we were eager to make the trip. We booked our flights for the following week.

The three of us went. When we arrived at the mother's house, Diana actually exclaimed, "Holy shit!" This was the biggest house we'd ever seen. It had to be 25,000 square feet. The mother and daughter greeted us at the door, and they were as charming as you could imagine. And they were very, very pleased to see us.

"Oh, my God! There you are!" They squealed as they opened the door. "All three of you!!" They were huge fans of the show and clearly delighted to see us.

I couldn't help but ask about the house and slip in the question, "What kind of work do you do?" I figured oil (it was Dallas, after all), but she said the family owned a chain of very popular restaurants. And yes, you've probably eaten at one of them.

The house was swanky, with columns, marble, huge rugs, and oil portraits on every wall. There were portraits of the husband, the wife, of the husband and the wife; portraits of the daughter, the son, the whole family; and portraits of dogs. As we walked through the house, they showed us at least six portraits of English Springer Spaniels. "Those are our beloved puppies," she said. "We are big fans of the Bushes, and they always had Springer Spaniels, so that's what we have, too."

They were talking a mile a minute, asking us questions about the show and other closets we had done. They were adorable and completely enamored of us. Dallas led us to a big room in the back where her and her daughter's things were. They wanted to stay with us while we decided what to buy, which makes it tricky for us because we like to be alone so we can decide, usually very quickly, what we will take. But Dallas and her daughter were not going to miss one second of the *Resale Royalty* experience. They were not going to leave our sides.

As it turned out, this was the one of the easiest closet buys we've ever done, because the items they had were *exactly* what we look for. Clothes from Theory, Vince, Alice and Olivia, Joie, Lululemon, Tory Burch, Lilly Pulitzer, and Anthropologie. And the volume was insane; they had dozens of practically new items to sell us. In addition to the clothes, they had four brand-new Louis Vuitton handbags to sell.

But the shoes and boots were the real standouts. They were all sizes 8 and 9, the most popular sizes, and they were all fabulous and easy sells: Jimmy Choo, Taryn Rose, Tory Burch, Frye, Eileen Fisher, Manolo Blahnik, Chanel, and twelve pairs of Louboutins. Louboutins are very sellable because they are so iconic, but nobody can wear them, so they never get worn out. Women love to buy them, then they resell them because they're the most uncomfortable shoe there is. Every day, people come in the Vault and say, "Oh, my God. I paid $1,200 for these shoes, but I can't wear them." And we buy them, resell them immediately, and the cycle continues.

Dallas and her daughter were shoppers. Most of their items still had the price tags on them. I could tell that they bought in bulk and could easily imagine a shopping trip to Neiman's or Nordstrom where they bought dozens of blouses and dresses, never to wear them.

When we do a closet buy, the girls and I go through every item together and then we each write down our total figure. We are always within $200 of each other. Always. It's amazing. It's particularly amazing because a lot of things are obscure. But what it comes down to is this: It's not how much the items cost, it's what we can sell them for.

We made an offer on about 200 items, and Dallas and her daughter were fully on board. We gave them our figure and they were thrilled. "Wowza!" they said in unison.

We loaded everything up, drove to the nearest UPS store, boxed everything, and shipped it back to Saint Louis. That was going to be a very, very profitable closet buy. I was happy to be with my daughters and proud of the great way we worked together.

Late that afternoon, I took Diana and Laura to a lovely lunch and surprised them with a pop-in to the Hermès store in Highland Park, where I bought us all matching bracelets. Even though we are the resale queens, sometimes a girl has to live a little and pay retail.

What about Bob?

When we are getting ready to do a closet, just before we walk out the door, we look at each other and say, "What about Bob? Where's Bob? Who's got Bob?"

Bob is not an employee or another McCarthy child. Bob is the Buy-Out Bag, and he goes everywhere we go. Bob is an old, roomy Chanel tote, and he holds everything we need for a closet buy: rubber bands (to band the hangers together), scrap paper, pens, calculator, checks, business cards, and sturdy paper shopping bags (we like the thick, high-quality ones from Sephora, Kate Spade, and Tory Burch). The minute we get back from a closet buy, Bob is replenished with supplies, so he's always ready to go. We never do a buy without Bob!

Chapter Ten

Mrs. Miller and the Hot Mess

W e look at about 1,000 pieces a day at our store in Saint Louis, so if we're going to travel to do a closet buy, there have to be a lot of shoes, jewelry, and handbags, as well as clothes. We won't travel exclusively for clothes, but we will cross the country—and fly abroad—for the promise of great handbags. Handbags bring us the most money. They are in high demand, and, because we know which bags to buy, they are a reliable profit center. Our top sellers are Chanel, Gucci, Coach, Marc Jacobs, Kate Spade, Tory Burch, and, the king of all, Louis Vuitton. We want classics and current styles, and we're always on the lookout for those great bags that are impossible to find.

One day as we were preparing for a trip to New York, I got a call from a woman in Manhattan. She said she was a friend of one of our very best clients and wondered if we'd be interested in doing her closet. The client she mentioned was a very good supplier for us, so the chances were excellent that this woman had good items, too. I took her info and gave it to Diana for prequalifying.

Diana called her and was super-excited. The woman, let's call her Mrs. Miller, had at least six handbags that she was hoping to sell, and Diana knew that these weren't your run-of-the-mill everyday bags. Diana told her we were heading to New York in a few days, and they made an appointment for our first day there. She gave Diana a swanky Central Park address, and we got ready for our trip.

We didn't recognize her name, so as soon as we got off the phone, we Googled her. Blammo: She was one of New York's biggest socialites with a very well-known hedge fund husband. We found oodles of pictures of her at every charity gala you can imagine: the New York Public Library, Sloan-Kettering, the Met Ball. This woman was high on the pecking order, and Diana and I couldn't wait to get into her closet.

When our flight landed, we were heading to baggage check when we saw a black-suited driver holding a card with my name on it.

I walked up to him and said, "Excuse me, I'm Sue McCarthy. Are you here for me?"

"Yes ma'am," he replied with the utmost courtesy. "Mrs. Miller sent me to collect you."

That was an unexpected surprise! We got our bags and got in the Town Car. I was worried because it was only 9 a.m. and our appointment with Mrs. Miller wasn't until 11 a.m. The driver said, "Mrs. Miller said to take you to your hotel and wait while you check in and freshen up, then bring you to her." What service!

We checked in at our hotel, freshened up, grabbed Bob the Buy-Out Bag, and headed downstairs, where the driver was waiting for us. The driver dropped us off, and we headed upstairs to the most incredible apartment, with sweeping views of the park and vaulted ceilings like something out of a movie. It was incredible: modern art on the walls, bespoke furniture everywhere, and a kitchen bigger than my house in Saint Louis.

Mrs. Miller met us at the door and was as sweet as can be. She was from Georgia, a real Southern belle. In her late forties or early fifties, she was beautifully coiffed and meticulously attired in a vintage Dior skirt and blouse, Chanel drop earrings, and Prada pumps. It was 11 a.m. and she was dressed to the nines. I liked this woman.

She ushered us into her apartment, and before we knew it, our coats had been taken and we had glasses of sparkling water in our hands. That famous Southern hospitality came through, and she made us feel like we were the most important people in the world. She led us on a tour of the apartment, and—I swear—if she hadn't been with us, we'd have never found our way out. The place was huge. She finally led us back to a closet that was probably 700 square feet—enormous.

"I want to show you some of my favorite things," she said. The clothes in the closet were mostly vintage, gorgeous, and in extraordinary condition. But we don't do vintage, so Diana and I started to get a little nervous. Just then a woman came into the room and said, "Mrs. Miller, lunch is ready."

"Wonderful," she said. "Ladies, please follow me." Mrs. Miller led us onto a patio with a fabulous view, where a maid served us a lovely lunch of poached lobster with, of course, champagne.

We chatted like old friends. Mrs. Miller was in no hurry, and she wanted to know all about our business, our clients, and the TV show. She wanted to know whose closets we were doing. Of course, we couldn't tell her who'd we bought from, but we did talk about the wonderful items we'd bought over the years. Her personal assistant joined us at the end of the meal, and Mrs. Miller excused herself.

The assistant led us to a room even larger than the vintage room. It was a beautiful walk-in closet, done up in pale peach with ivory accents, glass shelves, a silk daybed, and beautiful shoes, purses, jewelry, clothes, and—as we had hoped—handbags.

The assistant said, "Mrs. Miller said everything in this closet is available. Please take your time and let me know if you need anything. I will leave you to it."

Diana and I smiled like kids in a candy store—a really, really nice candy store. Her clothes were in perfection condition, and all the best labels: Armani, Chanel, Dior, Yves Saint Laurent, Lela Rose, Tom Ford. I knew that we were going to end up with lots and lots of clothes from this buy.

But the handbags were the best. It quickly became apparent that Mrs. Miller was old money. Her clothes and purses didn't scream money; they whispered sophistication, elegance, and quality. No Louis Vuitton bags splattered with the interlocking LV logos (which is actually our best seller). Bags like that say, "I've got money," but Mrs. Miller's bags said, "I've got money and I don't need giant logos to prove it." We picked fifteen that were just outstanding: a Givenchy, several Bottega Venettas, three Célines, a Goyard, two Prada, two Lady Diors, two Chanel Kelly bags, and—the best of all!—an Hermès Birkin bag.

All in all, we chose everything in that closet: the fifteen handbags, about seventy-five items of clothing, thirty items of jewelry (some fabulous Chanel that people had already seen her in so she couldn't wear again), thirty pairs of shoes (which were all the usual, wonderful suspects: Manolo, Chanel, Stuart Weitzman, and Prada), and a few scarves and belts. This shaped up to be one of our best buys ever. The purses alone made the trip! We wanted everything in that closet, literally.

We wanted to be sure our offer not only said how appreciative we were, but that we wanted to be invited back. We called the assistant back in and said we were ready to make an offer. I like to have the seller go first, so I said, "Thank you so much for allowing us this opportunity. We'd like to take everything. Do you have some idea of what Mrs. Miller wants for her things?"

The assistant said, "Mrs. Miller knows you are the experts. She completely trusts you and is pleased to be doing business with you. Just come up with a figure and let me know."

Now our mission is to impress Mrs. Miller, because what we want is to be invited back, so we offered a little more than we initially would have. The assistant said, "That sounds fine" and left to report to Mrs. Miller. She returned a minute later and said, "Mrs. Miller is thrilled. In fact, she is over the moon." That's what we want: clients who are over the moon.

I wrote a check for Mrs. Miller and told the assistant that we'd need some time to take everything out. The assistant said, "Oh no, we will box everything and ship it to you in Saint Louis. You don't have to do a thing."

The assistant led us back through the apartment to an office where Mrs. Miller was having tea with some friends.

"Oh, here they are!" she exclaimed when we entered the

room. "I was just telling my friends about how wonderful you are and how exciting this is! Ladies, you won't believe how much money they just paid me!"

She was thrilled, and thrilled to introduce us to her friends, who all said that they would call us when they were ready to part with their things. It was a love fest, and we were so pleased with how well everything had turned out.

"Now, what are you doing for dinner?" Mrs. Miller asked. "I don't want to be presumptuous, but I've made you a reservation at Per Se, and it's my treat. Please don't say no." We were stunned. "Now, my driver will take you wherever you need to go," she said. "And he will stay with you for the afternoon and evening and take you back to your hotel after dinner." We were blown away by the incredible hospitality. Now *we* were over the moon!

Mrs. Miller didn't need our money, and she didn't need to be so gracious and generous to us either. She could have been strictly transactional. But she wanted to do business with us because she liked us and had seen the show. She probably donated the money to charity, which is what a lot of our very wealthy clients do.

When people are that gracious, it's because they were raised well and know how to treat people. That was one of the best closet buys of all time and one of the most gracious and generous encounters we've ever had. The next day, however, was different.

While we were having dinner at Per Se, Diana received a phone call from a woman who identified herself as a close friend of one of our best clients, a celebrity stylist and fashion maven in New York. The woman said she was also a stylist and had just been talking to our mutual friend, who suggested she give us a call. She knew we were in town and wondered if we could swing by and look at her closet. Since this woman was a friend of our very good client, we were prepared to take it on faith that our time would be well spent. Plus, Diana said the woman dropped all the right names: Gucci, Fendi, Tom Ford, Chanel, and more. And we love to work with stylists, who usually become both great buyers and suppliers. Diana told her that we could see her the next morning at 9 a.m. That would give us enough time to ship any items we bought from her back to Saint Louis before heading to the airport for our 2 p.m. flight. The woman agreed, and we made the appointment.

The next morning, Diana and I were up bright and early, packed and ready. We hired a car to drive us to the woman's apartment in Hell's Kitchen, and we told the driver to wait for us with our luggage. We got out and rang the buzzer for her apartment (no doorman). No answer. We rang again. No answer. And again. No answer. And again. And we waited.

Diana called her. "Hi, there. It's Diana and Sue. We are downstairs, ready for our appointment with you. Call me back!" We waited about ten minutes. Still nothing. We walked to the Starbucks on the corner, got a coffee, waited ten minutes, then walked back. We tried buzzing again. No answer. We tried calling again. No answer.

We were about to leave when someone came out of the building. We grabbed the door, headed in, found her apartment, and rang her bell. Nothing. We rang again. Nothing. At this point, we were really irritated. But then the door opened a crack, and two bleary, bloodshot eyes, smudged raccoon-like with the previous night's mascara, peeked out from behind the chain.

"What?" she demanded hoarsely.

"Oh, hi there!" Diana said brightly. "Sorry to bother you. It's Diana Ford and Sue McCarthy. We had an appointment with you at 9 a.m. It's almost 9:30, and we thought we would just come up."

The young woman stared at us blankly for a very long minute, closed her eyes, and then closed the door. Diana and I looked at each other like, "Okaaaay…" But then the chain slid back, the door opened, and she said, "Come."

This girl was a hot mess. She had obviously been out late partying. She looked like something left over from Studio 54. She was beautiful though, tall and slim, with long, dark, bed-head hair. She was wearing a chic (and very wrinkled) silk kimono.

We stood there for what felt like an eternity. No one said anything. She looked at us like she had no idea who we were or why we were there, so Diana refreshed her memory.

"Your friend April gave you our info, and we are so glad you contacted us to come see your things. We do so much business with April, and we are thrilled to meet you." That seemed to jog her back to consciousness.

"Oh yes, the closet thing you guys do. Right. OK. Over here." And she led us across her postage-stamp size studio to her "closet," an area that had been cordoned off by a heavy velvet curtain.

The Hot Mess pulled aside the curtain to reveal a long rack of clothes and six shelves of shoes. Pinned to the items were the names of celebrities who had worn them, along with the date and the event. I touched one of the name tags and said, "Is this one of your clients?"

The Hot Mess said, "Yes, and all of these as well."

These celebrities were *huge*. One of the dresses I recognized immediately from the Oscars the year before. It was a stunning floor-length dress with delicate all-over beading.

"What an incredible dress," I said. "I remember when (insert name of famous actress) wore it. It was on the cover of every magazine. She looked incredible in it."

The Hot Mess agreed. "She is gorgeous, and she did look fabulous, but she has terrible ankles, so we always have to cover her feet." The Hot Mess perked up then and went dress by dress, dishing on the celebrities who had worn them.

It was fun to hear her dish, but with a car waiting downstairs and a flight to catch, we wanted to get down to business. So I asked her if these were the items she wanted us to look at to buy. "What do you mean buy?" she said. Oh, boy. It suddenly became apparent that she didn't know what we did or what was going on. I explained to her what we did, what a closet buy was, and why we were there.

"Oh, right, OK," she said. "Hmmm. I don't know."

I wondered if she thought we had come all the way across town just to see her closet. I was sure our very good client and her mutual friend had prepped her, but maybe the partying the night before had scrambled her brain a bit. She wasn't ready for us, she didn't understand what we did, and it was a little awkward. So, I said, "Look, thank you so much for seeing us, but if this isn't right for you, we can just head out."

But she said, "No, I understand. OK, let me pull some things out." And she started to go through her closet. A lot of the items she pulled out had obviously been used for recent editorial photo shoots. They were fabulous and very current, but they were so fashion-forward that we couldn't use them. That's not really our market, and we explained to her the things that we sold. She then pulled out a gorgeous floor-length Diane von Furstenberg dress.

"Here's one for you," she said. "I paid $900 for it so I want at least $800." Oh, boy. Here comes the tutorial.

I told her the dress was gorgeous, and we would love to have it. "At our store, we would sell that for $399, so I can offer you $200."

"That's crazy!" she said. "It's a $900 dress!" I gently told her that it *used* to be a $900 dress, but that it was now a $399 dress. In order for me to make a profit, I could only buy it for $200 or so.

This went on for the first few items or so, but once she understood our business model, we sailed through the rest of her closet and then moved on to the shoes. She had fabulous shoes. Some were a little too editorial for us, but she did have some very sellable Gucci sandals, Prada pumps, and, of course, Jimmy Choos. She then led us to her kitchen, and it was obvious that this was a woman who did not cook. (We didn't look in the fridge, but I am sure it contained only coconut water, pressed juice, and champagne.) Every surface was covered in bags, shoes, jewelry, and other accessories. On top of her stove were metal racks filled with dozens and dozens of clutches and small bags, probably over 100 of them: Judith Lieber, Yves

Saint Laurent, Louis Vuitton, Chanel, Marc Jacobs, Prada — every label you can imagine.

She ended up parting with several of her clutches, and we were ready to make the deal for about twenty items. By now, she understood how we operated, so we were pretty confident with our offer. But she said, "Oh, I was hoping to be here," and gave us a counter offer.

It wasn't that much more than what we had offered, so we said, "If that makes you happy, we will go there for you."

Done. And she was very happy. That is something we always want to do: make our clients happy, even if it means we take a little less. We won't leave until we can make them happy, as long as we can make our money. And on the very rare occasions when we can't make someone happy, we just don't take the items.

In the end, we bought shoes by Jimmy Choo, Prada, and Chanel; the DVF dress, a Prada dress, a Miu Miu dress, a YSL shirt, a Chanel skirt and belt, a Gucci belt; a Chanel clutch, a Chanel tote, a Louis Vuitton envelope clutch, two Judith Lieber metallic clutches, an Yves Saint Laurent clutch, and a few other things. All in all, it was a pretty good buy, absolutely worth our time, an interesting experience, and a good contact to make.

We packed up our purchases, and, as we were leaving, we noticed a huge painting propped against a wall. It was a painting of a birthday cake, signed, in huge letters, "Happy Birthday, darling! Love, Karl." That would be Karl Lagerfeld. The woman may have been a hot mess, but she was the real deal, fashion-wise.

Alex Carroll (past president of NARTS), me, and Patti Aquisto, the grande dame of the resale industry, 1990

Parking lot sale at Woman's Closet Exchange. All proceeds went to a women's shelter, 2002

Staff holiday party, 2005

The Vault, packed full of luxury clothing and accessories, 2014

Chapter Eleven
Less Is More and Words of Wisdom

I n 2016, I made a huge decision: I sold Women's Closet Exchange. When we opened the Vault Luxury Resale in 2014 and moved the Purple Cow there, we decided that Laura and Diana would run the Vault and I would stay at WCE. This worked well for a while. The Vault was doing phenomenally well under Diana and Laura's management, and I had a great manager helping me at WCE, someone who had been with me for ages. But I missed seeing and working with my daughters every day, and I was growing weary of the hours, the schlepping between the two stores, and the work load. Both stores were doing well, so why was I still killing myself?

I decided to take stock of my life. I was also about to turn seventy, so the time was right to ask myself what I really wanted to do and what really mattered.

I decided what I really wanted was to semi-retire. I didn't want to run WCE anymore, I didn't need two stores, and I wanted to be with my daughters. I decided that less is more, and so I sold WCE to my manager, who jumped at the chance to buy me out.

I was now free to focus solely on the Vault, be with my daughters, do some closet buys, attend events, travel with Larry, and generally slow down a bit. Without the worries and pressures of owning two stores, I was freer and able to do more in life. It's the best decision I've made in ages, and I couldn't be happier.

The Vault is now my world, and my vision—the one I had way back in 1991 when I opened my first 400-square-foot store—has been perfectly realized. We have turned it into an incredible place. It's a store and an event space rolled into one. It's a place for friends to gather, drink wine, and shop. It's a place for fashion shows and charity events. It's a place for stylists to come and shop for their clients.

Our mission statement is painted right there on the wall when you walk in: "Nurturing women through fashion and inspired events." And that's the truth. The Vault isn't just a store; it's a place for women to be together and become their best selves. Fashion is serious business, and it is very, very meaningful. It's like Nigel said in the movie *The Devil Wears Prada*: "Fashion is more important than art because you live your life in it." It's beauty *and* art. It's pleasure *and* power. It's purpose *and* pride.

Clothes and accessories have a tremendous impact on how you feel about yourself and how other people see you. They can make you feel strong, confident, powerful, and attractive—or uncomfortable, constricted, and self-conscious. Our job is to make available the most beautiful things in the world at affordable prices. Our job isn't to sell you stuff; it's to help you look and feel your best, which we do with honesty and integrity. If you try something on and it's not right, you will hear a chorus of honest women: "Nope. That's not right for you. Take it off!" We provide an affordable way for women to look and feel great. And there is nothing frivolous about that.

My daughters and I love working together to bring women the best things we can find. We will go from coast to coast and overseas to find the best items for our customers. We love our customers, and we love what we do. And we take it seriously. We want to make fashion fun, accessible, and affordable. We want to help every woman look great, feel great, and be great, sizes 00-22.

I have loved every minute of my life so far, and I am so proud of the resale businesses my daughters and I have built. I feel proud and blessed to have achieved so much and so honored to have helped so many women look and feel their best.

I may not be Bill Gates, but I think I'm a pretty successful business woman. I get to work with the people I love most in the world, in an industry that has real meaning and impact. I get to travel and meet new people all over the world. I get to help bring women together and help them feel great about themselves. And financially, we've done pretty well. I am full of gratitude every day.

People always ask me for business advice. They want to know how to be successful. To me, the road to success is paved with the same stones, no matter the endeavor. Here are my top ten tips:

1. Integrity is everything.

If you don't have integrity, you may be profitable, but you won't be successful. To me, integrity is the cornerstone of success. Integrity means doing what you say you are going to do. Integrity means being fair and honest. That's the simplest business model in the world and the secret to success: Do what you're supposed to do, do it well, do it fairly, and do it honestly.

2. Have passion for what you are doing.

Anyone who wants to start a business must have passion for what they want to do. You might be successful, but you won't be happy.

Passion makes the hours fly by. It never feels like work if you're passionate about what you're doing. That's the secret. If you love what you do, you never *have* to go to work; you *get* to go to work.

That's why I've been in this business so long: because I'm absolutely passionate about it. I love the clothes. I love fashion. I love how it changes. I love helping women find affordable luxury. I love the community of women around our business, and I love helping women feel good about themselves. For me, upscale resale fires on all cylinders.

3. Always do the right thing.

You know *exactly* what the right thing is. Don't put a few dollars ahead of your ethics, morals, or sense of fairness. Don't put profit ahead of kindness, generosity, and consideration. In business, you'll be faced with many situations where doing the right thing might mean less money in your pocket. It might mean an extra effort, an unforeseen expense, or a loss of some sort. But I guarantee you that if you err on the side of kindness, consideration, and generosity, you'll come out ahead.

For me, doing the right thing always yields a far more positive outcome. Here's a simple example. A few years ago, a good regular customer came in looking for a dress for her daughter's wedding. We had just gotten in a lovely pale grey shift dress with some sparkly beading on the neckline. The dress was brand new, never worn, with the price tags still on it. The retail price of the dress was $199, and our price was $89. The woman tried it on, fell in love with it, and bought it. Perfect.

Two months later, she came into the store and told us that she had been shopping at Macy's and saw the same dress on sale for $59, marked down from $199. She asked us for the price difference of $30.

My first reaction was, "Are you crazy? That's a $200 dress that we sold to you for $89, and now you want us to discount it even further?"

Then I thought it through. She had been a valued client for a long time, and we were surprised that she would even request such a thing. But in her mind, it was a problem, and it was obviously very important to her. I took my emotion out of it and thought about it from her perspective. What would it cost me to make this right? We commiserated with her situation and gave her a $30 store credit. She spent the credit in our store (and then some!), we kept a good client, and it cost us only our time to listen and a small credit.

Don't think about dollars. Think about what will make your client or customer happy. The right thing to do may not always be the most profitable thing to do, but if you can make things right for your customers, you'll be successful.

4. Never think you know everything.

I've been in this business for twenty-six years, I'm a highly paid consultant in the resale industry, and I speak at conferences around the country. But I never, ever assume that I know more than anyone else or that I have nothing left to learn. I constantly seek out new people for new ideas both within and outside my industry.

If you think you know everything, you can't learn; and if you can't learn, you can't grow and succeed. Be humble and listen. Just because you're a success doesn't mean that you can't learn new and better ways to do things. And if you're just starting out, cast a wide net, ask questions, and listen. You never know where you'll find that next great idea or inspiration, or from whom you'll learn it.

5. Embrace change.

When I first started, there was no Internet, no Facebook, no email. I was advertising in the phone book and on grocery carts! Things grow and change so quickly—technology, fashion, marketing—that if you don't embrace change, you won't succeed. Change is a success agent, and it goes hand in hand with being open, listening to new ideas, and learning from other people.

6. Treat customers like queens and surprise them with thoughtful touches.

Our customers are our lifeblood. Without them, there is no business. The customer comes first, always, and we constantly look for ways to knock their socks off, to go above and beyond niceties. We bend over backwards to make their experiences wonderful, to provide lovely moments for them every time they come to our stores, to give them a little something extra—*lagniappe*!

We greet them immediately, and when we say "hello" and "welcome," we really mean it. We offer service, but we will stay in the background if that suits your style. We treat everyone with respect. We want to establish a relationship with the customer, no matter who they are.

And that's another very, very important point: we are gracious with every single person who walks in our door. It doesn't matter if the person is dripping with Chanel or wearing Target sweatpants with two screaming kids in tow. Our customers are all queens in our eyes. We want to do business with everyone, so everyone gets the same royal treatment.

7. Manage expectations and educate gently.

A lot of education goes on in the resale business, and the "lessons" must be delivered gently but firmly to our suppliers. On very rare occasions, sellers become upset when they want to sell their items and their prices are out of line with what we're able to pay, so sometimes we have to educate them and manage their expectations.

One of the ways we do that is by asking them what they are hoping to get for their items. We want to find out where they are in their thinking, so we know where they are emotionally. Before we make our offer, we will ask, "What were you hoping to get today?" Then we can discuss the realities of resale buying and where we are price-wise. We are always very polite and courteous, because we truly want them to understand how it works.

Once the seller understands the mechanics of our business, she's better prepared, and we can discuss the offer.

And it's going to be a fair offer, based on what we think we can get for her items and what we can give her so that we can still make a profit. By managing expectations and educating sellers to the realities of resale, we can turn them into good clients.

8. Be careful not to bruise egos.

I'd never advocate lying to a customer. Being fair and honest is the cornerstone of my business. That said, sometimes a little blurring of the truth is necessary to avoid hurt feelings and bruised egos.

We had a woman in recently, about my age, who had the attitude that she was much too good to do business with us. She had heard from friends that we sold luxury items, and she brought in some things for us to look at. She only wanted to sell her stuff and, at first, wouldn't even look on our sales floor. But we like to take our time and practice due diligence when we appraise items, so we encouraged her to stroll the floor while we looked at her items.

Her items were very good labels, but they were old and worn, too much for us to sell. I called her back when I was ready, and I graciously told her that I wasn't able to buy any of her items that day. She got very upset and said, "Well, I'll tell you something. My things are better than anything you have in this store!"

I said, "Oh, that's absolutely true! Your things are much better than anything we'd ever consider having here. You obviously have excellent taste, and your items are obviously well- loved."

Then I lowered my voice and leaned in close to her. "But you know, people today, they just don't want to buy the older items. Your items are fabulous, but I'm afraid that I won't be able to resell them to my clients. But if you ever have anything that's a bit newer and less well-loved, please try us again."

She softened visibly. I had validated her feelings about her taste and her items, and I was able to diffuse her temper and arrogance. I didn't want her leaving and then saying bad things about us. (The only time we ever get bad reviews is when we turn down items.)

You can't always make people happy, but it is absolutely worth every effort to try—even if there is no sale involved and even if you have to fudge the truth a bit and massage a few egos. Do what it takes to make every customer's experience a positive one, even if they don't buy or sell anything.

9. Treat your staff well.

Your customers are your lifeblood, but your staff keeps your business pumping. Do right by your employees, and they will do right by you.

We take great pride in the way we operate. We pay well—actual living wages!—and we offer generous benefits and bonuses. We treat our staff with respect, listen to their views and suggestions, and take their input seriously.

We're conscious of the bottom line, of course. So on certain special shopping days, we will pay bonuses to everyone working when we hit storewide sales numbers. *Everyone* working that day gets a bonus: the woman working the register, the buyers in the back, the fitting room attendant, and the people on the floor.

It takes a team to do it right, and we reward everyone equally. There's incentive for everybody to do a good job, and it's not competitive. It's teamwork.

Beyond good salaries, benefits, and bonuses, offering your employees flexibility and support is also very important. I'm a wife and mother, and my family comes first. I have always told my employees that their families come first as well. Our staff is all female, and we all know that the bulk of family work falls to women.

We tell our staff, "If your kid is sick, you take off, and we will cover for you as long as we have to. Nobody is ever going to make you feel bad or guilty. If you have an emergency in the family, you take off as long as you need to."

We are generous, fair, and flexible with our employees, and you should be, too. But be sure to separate friendship from business. I am friendly and loving and supportive and generous with my employees, but I make it clear that I am the boss. You must be able to make that distinction, and you must be able to do what needs to be done in the best interest of your business. It is very hard to have a difficult conversation with—or, God forbid, fire—a friend, so always maintain that bright line between boss and employee.

10. Give back to your customers and your community.

I believe in giving back. I believe in good works, charity, and compassion. I believe in gratitude. And that is why we give back to our customers through special events and promotions. Of course, we want them to shop, but we also genuinely want to thank them for being customers. So we offer champagne, coffee, cupcakes, and chocolates. We host wine tastings and tea parties, fashion shows and book signings.

We are firmly rooted in the belief that you must give back to your community, so we also host fundraisers and community events and make direct donations to charities. We take that responsibility seriously. Over the years, we've donated over $250,000 to charities. In 2017 alone, we raised over $45,000 at the Vault for local charities, including Helping Hand-Me-Downs, the Institute for Family Medicine, Forest Park Forever, the World Pediatric Project, the National Council of Jewish Women, and other organizations and individuals.

Yes, it's good business, but it's also our way of participating in our wider world and being caring, compassionate, and generous. What good is success if you can't help your world be a better place?

A Little Something Extra:

Getting the most bang for your buckskins

We pride ourselves on paying very well and very fairly for merchandise. Here's advice on how to get the best price for your items.

1. Presentation is everything.

First and foremost, the better your items look, the more money you're going to get. So before you bring them in, take a good look at them and prepare them so that they look as close to the day you bought them as possible. The closer your garment, shoes, handbag, jewelry, or accessories look to new, the more money you're going to get.

If your items are tossed into boxes or garbage bags, they will not show well. Put your clothes on hangers, and if the hangers all match and are going in the same direction, that is terrific. Make it easy for us to see how nice your things are. Remove dry cleaning bags and tags.

Make sure that your garments are clean and free of wrinkles, the hems are pressed and stitched, and buttons are sewn on. We will pass on items that have stains, missing buttons, or ripped hems or seams.

Make sure that shoes and handbags are clean. We don't

want to look inside a purse and find gum wrappers. Clean and polish the leather and buff out scuffs. We don't want shoes that look worn, with scuff marks and ragged heels. Make sure there is no dirt on the heels or soles of shoes.

2. Save your receipts, tags, and bags.

This is especially important with high-end handbags, shoes, and jewelry. We authenticate every item we sell, so save everything that can help verify authenticity. Oftentimes, high-end bags and shoes come inside a larger, softer bag, and then in a box. Save those and bring them. Bags are usually accompanied by little ID or care cards; save those, too.

If you have the original receipts, bring them with you. Knowing where and when you purchased your Louis Vuitton bag makes you a more credible seller and makes our job easier. If you have the box, the card, the bag, and the receipt, it literally makes your item three times more valuable to us. Authentication is paramount in our business; the more documentation you have, the better—and the more money you're going to get.

3. Don't cut the labels out.

If you ever plan to resell your clothes, do not cut the labels out. I know they can sometimes be itchy and annoying, but they are important. Authenticity and origin are very important to us and essential to our business. Leave the labels in.

4. Beware a price tag.

If your item is brand new and still has the price tags on it, that's great. But I always tell my buyers: Beware price tags. If something has a price tag on it, that means somebody bought it and never wore it; and if it was never worn, there's probably a reason. Maybe they buy so many things that they never got around to wearing it or returning it. But maybe the item is mis-sized, unflattering, or uncomfortable.

Just because it still has a price tag doesn't mean it's a great find. We recently bought a beautiful sequined Eileen Fisher dress with the price tag still on it—$499 retail. It was stunning, and we bought it the second the seller showed it to us. But we have not been able to sell the darn thing because it's itchy. It looks great and hangs great and is the perfect thing to wear over a pair of leggings for a dressy night out. But after about ten seconds, the sequins make you itch like crazy. Every person who tries it on says the same thing. Just because you paid $400 for something doesn't mean we will be able to sell it, either.

5. Do your homework.

Don't come in thinking you're going to get retail for your item. Before you come in, go online and check out a few sources. Let's say you have a Chanel bag. Now, you can find ten of those Chanel bags online, and the seller is going to ask for whatever they want. Five of them are going to ask outrageous prices. But check out the people who have been in business for a long time and who are reputable, and see what their prices are. Then cut that in half, because that's what you're going to get from us. I'm going to resell your handbag, and I have to make a profit. The good thing about doing business with us is that you immediately walk away with cash in your hand. Selling online is great, except when it's not. So do your homework before you come to the store.

6. Stay on top of trends.

Right now, ath-leisure is our biggest seller. We can't get enough of it, and it flies off the racks. But three years ago? Not so much. Fifteen years ago, we couldn't get enough suits. Now? We won't buy a suit because we can't give it away. You may have paid $600 for that high-end suit because you had an interview, but no one else wants it.

Make sure you know what is selling and what is not so you'll know what to bring. Come in and take a look around to see what we have on the floor. And ask questions.

More than any other resale shop in the country, we are very current with trends. We parallel the industry. If it isn't current and in style, we have no use for it.

7. Accessories are always hot.

Shoes, purses, and jewelry are our biggest sellers, as long as they are current, which means in the past two years. Those are go-to items for a lot of women, and we can sell them fast.

8. Come to sell any day but Saturday.

Don't come to sell your items on a Saturday. Saturday is our busiest day, followed by Monday and Friday. Those are the days when we take in the most items, so we are less likely to take as much time with yours. Come on a day when we can take more time with your items—Tuesday, Wednesday, or Thursday.

9. Sell out of season.

The best time to sell clothes is out of season. If it's 105 degrees outside, we aren't buying shorts and sundresses; we are buying for fall and winter. Like stores, we buy preseason. Getting your spring and summer items in the store in January and February will almost guarantee that you'll get top dollar. When the whole world is wearing parkas, bring in your shorts. Call first and ask what we are buying.

10. Ask for more money and be open to store credit.

Finally, one of the best-kept secrets is that people often get more money when they simply ask for it. Any good buyer knows that in order to seal the deal, she may have to budge on her offer a bit. Usually there is a little wiggle room for us to meet in the middle. We want to be very fair, and we want our sellers to be happy. And you can always get more in store credit than in cash, so that's always an option, too.

Visit us!

The Vault Luxury Resale
2325 South Brentwood Blvd.
Brentwood, MO 63144

Telephone: 314-736-6511

On the web: thevaultluxuryresale.com
Instagram: @thevaultluxuryresale
Facebook: @thevaultluxuryresale

Sue McCarthy

Sue McCarthy is the founder and CEO of the Vault Luxury Resale, a multimillion-dollar resale boutique in Saint Louis. Sue and her daughters were the stars of *Resale Royalty*, a popular reality TV series produced by celebrity stylist Rachel Zoe that aired on the Style Network in 2013.

Sue has been in the upscale resale business for twenty-six years. She founded her first store, Women's Closet Exchange, in 1991, in a tiny 400-square-foot storefront. She pioneered the upscale resale business model, in which items are purchased outright rather than consigned from sellers, which represented a major shift from the traditional consignment business model.

Because of her savvy, sophisticated methods, business acumen, and incredible success, Sue is widely recognized as the doyenne of upscale resale. She is a frequent guest speaker at the annual conference of the National Association of Resale Professionals and has served as both vice president and board member.

Sue's mottos are "Beautiful things are meant to be shared" and "If it's not becoming on you, it should be coming to me."

Diana McCarthy Ford

Diana McCarthy Ford is the director of marketing and special events for the Vault and co-starred on *Resale Royalty*. Born and raised in Saint Louis, she is a graduate of Saint Louis University where she earned her bachelor's degree in marketing and communications. She worked as a concierge at the Ritz-Carlton in Clayton, Missouri, and as conference director at Maritz Travel. She has traveled to and planned events on all seven continents (yes, that includes Antarctica).

In 2005, Diana started The Shopping Co., which offers exclusive excursions to New York, Chicago, Scottsdale, London, and Paris. At the Vault, Diana plans and executes industry events, fashion shows, resale bus tours, VIP shopping, in-home trunk shows, and more, including book signings for fashion heavyweights like Fern Mallis, the founder of New York Fashion Week. Diana is a board member of the Saint Louis Fashion Fund and an accomplished stylist for photo shoots, fashion shows, and private clients.

Diana's mottos are "No is not an option" and "Just say no-no to so-so."

Laura McCarthy Maurice

Laura McCarthy Maurice is the chief curator, social media manager, and director of celebrity and out-of-town acquisitions for the Vault Luxury Resale. Along with her mother and sister, she co-starred on *Resale Royalty*.

Laura was born and raised in Saint Louis. She studied communications at the University of Missouri-Saint Louis and at Washington University in St. Louis and acting for the camera and voice-over at the Center of Creative Arts. She performed in local theater and did commercials for radio stations.

As chief curator, Laura oversees the buying of thousands of authentic luxury items a year from 15,000 suppliers around the world. She is a label savant and fashion guru who knows every brand and the retail cost of every item that comes in. Laura was a board member of the Saint Louis Fashion Fund. She is also an accomplished stylist for photo shoots and fashion shows, as well as a personal stylist for private clients.

Laura's mottos are "Fashion should be accessible to every woman" and "You've got to look good to feel good."